C'mon, Let's Play!

Living, playing and moving forward

DEE G. SUBERLA

BALBOA.PRESS
A DIVISION OF HAY HOUSE

This book is a work of non-fiction. Unless otherwise noted, the author and the publisher make no explicit guarantees as to the accuracy of the information contained in this book and in some cases, names of people and places have been altered to protect their privacy.

Balboa Press books may be ordered through booksellers or by contacting:

Balboa Press
A Division of Hay House
1663 Liberty Drive
Bloomington, IN 47403
www.balboapress.com
844-682-1282

Because of the dynamic nature of the Internet, any web addresses or links contained in this book may have changed since publication and may no longer be valid. The views expressed in this work are solely those of the author and do not necessarily reflect the views of the publisher, and the publisher hereby disclaims any responsibility for them.

The author of this book does not dispense medical advice or prescribe the use of any technique as a form of treatment for physical, emotional, or medical problems without the advice of a physician, either directly or indirectly. The intent of the author is only to offer information of a general nature to help you in your quest for emotional and spiritual well-being. In the event you use any of the information in this book for yourself, which is your constitutional right, the author and the publisher assume no responsibility for your actions.

Any people depicted in stock imagery provided by Getty Images are models, and such images are being used for illustrative purposes only. Certain stock imagery © Getty Images.

Print information available on the last page.

ISBN: 978-1-9822-4980-9 (sc)
ISBN: 978-1-9822-4982-3 (hc)
ISBN: 978-1-9822-4981-6 (e)

Library of Congress Control Number: 2020923920

Balboa Press rev. date: 12/04/2020

With love and gratitude, I dedicate this book to my beautiful and amazing friend Carole Lee White. She was my mentor, friend, and confidant. Her advice guided me through decades, and I am grateful. One of the last times I visited her, I told her about this book. She suffered from dementia, but we went on forever talking about the old days. I told her about leaving my job at Baxter and what I learned from that experience. She sat straight up, pointed at me, and shouted, "Put that in your book!" And so, I did. I hope you enjoy that section. At that point, I told her I would be dedicating the book to her. If you have time, check out the necklace she made; I was delighted when she gave it to me. You can see it in my picture on this book. Carole passed away in June 2019.

Thank you, Carole. I love and cherish you, my friend. I can't imagine what my life would have been like without your ever-present friendship and guidance.

CONTENTS

INTRODUCTION

I wrote this book to share ideas that might help you to figure out what you want out of life and to consider that your life is much more in your control than you ever imagined. Living an amazing life is not something you have to earn, the result of a lucky draw, or an entitlement established by ... well, whatever. It's not something that's only there for a chosen few. It's something you were born to do in a universe that is always helping you to get what you want.

"Oh no," you say? Well, once you awaken to the fact that there is a certain way to make requests of the universe, you'll realize it has all been a communications mistake, not a universal conspiracy to bring you misery. Requests made to the universe are not "May I please have ..." or "What did I do to deserve this?" It's what I call *intentional imagination*.

It works for me, and believe me when I tell you that I have had a lot of experience wandering around, bumping into and tripping over life, which resulted in getting a lot of what I didn't want. You and I are not alone in this practice, by the way.

Once I stumbled into these concepts, I was able to help myself. As a result, I experienced the thrill of freely living the amazing life that I had only imagined in the past. Yeah, I still stumble every now and again, and sometimes it takes me longer than it should to get back in the groove; but I get there!

These concepts come from everywhere, from every angle: business, spirituality, and self-help. I have distilled my favorite information so that others might begin the process. I hope you will use it as a guide to begin to define and live your amazing life. I have synthesized what worked for me into a step-by-step approach. It is time to claim a fulfilling life that serves your highest good and the highest good for others.

Yes, there is a process, and here is the "good news, bad news" part: it's the one you're following right now, every day with every breath. You may not have realized that, but from this point moving forward, you will no longer be able to claim that. Consider this your leaping-off point. So many wonderful people today, and throughout history, have described how to do it as a spiritual journey, a path to business success, or just a simpler way to live. The information available is vast, and it covers a lot of territory. I'm helping to bring the starting point into focus.

Think about where you'd like to step into a more fulfilling life: your job, romance, or relationships with friends or family? Perhaps it's by improving your self-esteem or becoming a better pet owner, artist, poet, or cook? This book is intended to help you find the way to freely express your passions, joys, and gifts.

Seriously, I don't know why this information isn't taught in grade school and high school. It would have been great if I had found it sooner, but I am grateful to have found it at all. Part of living the life that I love is being able to share this with you. I love sharing it!

I am proposing that you begin to follow this process intentionally, with purpose, and on purpose, because—and here's the spoiler—the alternative is that you continue to do it unconsciously, by default, while blaming the cruel world for all the lack and despair that you feel. (Take a dramatic pause and visualize me raising the back of my hand to my forehead.) "Oh, woe is me!"

Yes, devastating things happen sometimes and are nothing to joke about. I don't make light of those events, but I do make light of how often we act as if something horrific happened when *I was cut off in traffic by that idiot driver!* Or *I missed out on a great sale!* Or *I heard that someone said I'm fat and stupid!*

We might add up all these bad things and come to expect more bad things, and a cycle of unhappiness and a feeling of never having anything go right for us becomes fully justified. When things do go right, we tend not to notice them. We lie in wait for the next bad thing to happen, and when it does, we pounce on it, saying, "Aha! There it is! I knew something would go wrong!"

Look around. What do you see? What is going on in your life right now? If you're not that crazy about what you see, I have some great news for you! You can change it! Because of the way the universe works, creating the life that we want is something every single one of us does every single day. Like it or not! So, if your life is more about what you don't want, that is because you are spending a significant amount of your mental focus on what you don't want. Take it from the title of Dr. Wayne Dyer's eBook with Barnes and Noble: "You'll see it when you believe it!"[1]

The universe responds in a way I had never imagined. It responds to how we feel inside and to what we actually believe way down deep—at

---

[1] Wayne Dyer, *You'll See It When You Believer It: The Way to Your Personal Transformation* (HarperCollinsUS, 2010), Cover.

our core, that place where we think we're all alone and no one can see or hear. That's the very place where we connect with the universe. Yeah, that's right; I said it. The sooner you get it, the sooner you can get out of your own way and *help yourself* to create a life where you share your passions and find joy while serving a greater good!

Most people don't have any idea what a joy-filled life would look like. I sure didn't the first time I was asked to describe what mine looked like. A lot of people will begin describing how they would be happy if their children (or other family members) were happy. But this isn't about them; it's about you, just you. When was the last time you gave yourself a moment to reflect upon your good and to love yourself? Do this! I heard that groan a few of you just made. More on this later.

Many people simply acquiesce to the circumstances surrounding them and believe, "This is the way it is, and this is the way it will always be. There's nothing I can do about it." They believe it is a bad life because that's all they're entitled to, or because there is some unjust cause working against them. Wrong.

The reality is your life is what you make it through your own belief system. I once heard a great explanation of this. *It's all about your own BS!* (BS as in *belief system*.) Changing what you believe about your life changes your life. It changes *everything!* Change your belief and change your life!

Really, I promise. I know firsthand how hard it is to hear that we are each accountable for the way our lives are right now. For the most part, our lives are the result of our beliefs and the choices we made because of something that happened (or didn't happen) years ago. We believe, because it wasn't our fault, that we are victims of circumstances.

In the early days, I had a laundry list of the bad things that had happened to me along the way and how the negative impact of those things—which by the way, were completely out of my control—were why my life was so messed up. The condition of my life was not my fault! I thought I really was the victim because I am not a bad person. *It wasn't my fault!* And I absolutely did not ask for it in any way. I believed that what I saw around me was the true reality and that was that. No one would give me a chance to make things better. *Ha!* Turns out it wasn't a conspiracy; it was just me. Who knew?

If you are thinking that you are a victim of life or completely helpless to make things better for yourself right now, please, oh please, stay with me for a while longer. Here's the thing: it's not about blame; it's not about punishment. It's about moving forward. It's about using your power to free yourself of the anchors to which you have chained yourself. It's as though you have chained yourself to that time when you were truly a victim—and are, therefore, still a victim.

When we look at something horrible from the past and review it, remember it, and rely on it, we keep it alive-ish as a current part of our lives. It is a piece of expired history, but we prop it up, and like a pet zombie, it walks around the halls of our minds today, right now. It feels as if it happened yesterday or this morning. It didn't happen then, but you breathed life into then, and this morning too, maybe.

Explanations, blame, anger, and so many of the victimizing beliefs we have are the anchors. Our beliefs connected to them are the chains that bind us. You did not cause those bad things, but your reaction to them over time, and what you believe about them, has everything to do with the life you have right now. If this feels familiar, then this is where you are unconsciously using your power to cocreate a life you don't want.

Well, there it is, and you can't unknow it! Take this opportunity to think about how you can embrace your power and work with the blessings of the universe. It's an opportunity to become grateful every day. Gratitude is a magical elixir, even if it is over something as simple as finding a book like this in your hands. Or it can well up in us over a warm breeze, a butterfly, and of course, those amazing sunsets. Please join me. Come on. There's a lot to go over. Let's have fun with it. Let's play!

With love and gratitude,

Dee

Little Children

O little children in the street,
With dirty hands and naked feet,
I watch you run and skip and fall
And play catch with a big beach ball.

O little children in the park,
Who must go home when it gets dark,
I hear you laugh and sing and cry;
When night grows near, I hear you sigh.

O little children hard at play,
It is too bad you cannot stay.
Since I was once a child too,
May I come out and play with you?

C'mon, let's play!

CHAPTER 1

Me and My Numb Spots

One pill makes you larger, and one pill makes you small;
and the ones that mother gives you don't do anything at all.
—Grace Slick

I have numb spots in my brain. I'm always surprised when they take an active role in my life, being numb spots and all. Sometimes when something very dramatic happens, I don't feel things—mentally, physically, or emotionally. Of course, at other times you might find me weeping while watching puppies or a brilliant sunset.

Over the years, I've done a lot of research, learning and observing, and have integrated the best of it into this book to serve as an entry point for those looking for a way to move forward. I love knowing that my résumé, the work I do, my education, my financial circumstances, and my previous experiences do not define me. Nor do the roles I play in this world or any of those questionable choices I've made over the years (although many of those choices, as it turns out, make darn good stories!).

My questionable choices serve as great examples of how a person can transcend his or her circumstances and ignite his or her own power to live a life filled with wonder, beauty, and passion. For me, it's all about learning and moving forward—just moving forward in love and joy. When I discovered my purpose, I was so grateful that I could live the life that I wanted to live but felt disconnected from the possibility of it happening. And then I discovered my power, and quite honestly, it turns out we do have superpowers!

Hello, I'm Dee Suberla. I help people figure out what they really want in their lives, and then I help them get out of their own way so it can happen!

I believe we are all aspects of the same thing, lovely facets of a single jewel, separate waves on the ocean, clusters of particles in the same universal soup. I believe that because inside the real me and the real you—at our very cores—are those tiny specks that God blessed us with; some call them souls or spirits. Everything in the universe is connected—yes, including my numb spots.

This took me a while to learn or, more truthfully, to believe. Now I know that I'm here to engage life through the passions that drive me. Part of all this, in my case, is that I have numb spots due to the fact that I need them; they help me in my work, and I believe I access them during times when objectivity is required. Turns out they're quite useful.

So how does one go about developing numb spots? I think there must be a million ways. I believe that my original numb spots were there when I was born. I can remember occasionally spacing out at a very young age. The earliest memory of this was the time I forgot to put my hand down after a vote was over. Some of the parents in our neighborhood were creating a new club for girls my age. They asked for suggestions, and I suggested the name Us Guys. The lady in charge suggested we change it to Us Gals. By a show of hands, we voted and agreed. The name Us Gals won hands down—well, one hand was still up. I was talking to my girlfriend well after the vote was over, with that darn hand stuck up in the air like some sort of spaced-out flagpole.

"Put your hand down," my friend Toni whispered. For a second there, I looked up at it completely confused. *What the heck?* As I slid my hand down to my lap, I wondered how someone could forget something like that and became extremely concerned. I immediately imagined that all those nightmares about forgetting to get dressed before school could really come true.

The numb spots, which are actually ischemic scar tissue, are located around the base of my brain and my amygdala. The doctor suggested that as a cave woman, I would have had a short life because the scar tissue would have messed with my "fight, flight, or freeze" responses—key instincts that would have signaled the presence of a gigantic dinosaur and triggered flight.

I started smoking cigarettes in eighth grade, about a pack a week. As time went on, I discovered the joy of altered states. By sophomore year in high school, I discovered the magical properties of marijuana, white cross, and psilocybin. After graduation, I fell in love with prescription barbiturates and diet pills, and for a while, I continued my experimentation. I occasionally became one gigantic numb spot. I think I may have seen a dinosaur or two and tried to carry on a conversation— literally incapable of running at some points.

My guess is that the numb spots I was born with must have been filled with lost memories of the sense my parents knocked into me. And realistically, I probably created a few more with "experimentation." I

3

am grateful to be here to tell this story. Many of my classmates didn't make it. Ah, the seventies. I am truly a survivor!

I was the baby of the family. Mom and Dad had five children. They had the first three, and when the youngest was around twelve, my mother prepared to go to work as a Welcome Wagon lady. She had lovely black-and-white photos taken that I found decades later. She never got to experience the Welcome Wagon lady job because she got pregnant. My sister Suzie was born, and my parents immediately decided to have another baby so Suzie had a playmate. Yep, that's right. That was me; I was born to play. In retrospect, I might have pushed the envelope a bit on that one.

My amazing parents never had a chance with me, partially because they were the same age as my friends' grandparents. There was a brief period of time when they thought that I might be losing my mind and considered sending me away, but instead we went to a craft store, and they bought me a tiger-striped rug craft project. They even let me pick out different colors—my favorites, red and black. But what was really going on was that I had discovered a few things about becoming a hippie at thirteen, and my parents never imagined that I was turning into an addict. They thought that my ability to sit and stare at a wall for so long was an indication of extreme boredom hovering on madness. I was just stoned.

I usually refused to take aspirin or any over-the-counter pill that Mom offered when I wasn't feeling well, primarily because it seemed pointless; there was absolutely no recreational value. Mom was certain that I just didn't like to take pills of any kind, unlike so many of those wild kids she heard about on the nightly news.

My parents let us taste the liquor they kept in the liquor cabinet and told us if we ever wanted to drink that we should do it at home. It all tasted terrible to me, and as a result, Mom called me her little teetotaler. I was quite confident they would never figure out that I was a drug-crazed teen with a fake ID going to bars in a neighboring state—where I discovered the amazing elixir Lambrusco!

My sister and I were blessed with curly hair, but we thought it was some sort of cruel and unusual punishment. So we did the sensible thing and used Mom's iron and ironing board to straighten out each other's unruly locks. Then one day Mom showed me a picture of a girl in a magazine who had the same kind of hair as mine. But this girl had just split her hair down the middle and let it go wild. The magazine called it a *hairstyle!* It was wild, I loved it, and the text below the picture suggested that all the hippies were doing it! Then my amazing mother said these inspiring words to her very naughty thirteen-year-old baby girl: "Don't ever let me catch you doing this with your hair!"

I remember the first time I set my hair free and went out in public. I carefully selected an outfit to wear to the carnival. I chose my torn red, white, and blue–striped jeans, a navy-blue tank top, and my stars-and-stripes gym shoes. I finished the outfit off with a beautiful white fringed shawl that Mom had made for me. It was supposed to be dressy. It was shimmery, but I claimed it for this outfit. It had fringe, for crying out loud, and that made it perfect for this budding hippie! My friend and I wandered around the carnival doing our best to look cool, and then she gave me the most amazing compliment. "Dee, you really do look like a hippie."

I'd made it! I may have worn that exact outfit for a month, and yes, it was washed regularly. Mom did have some very firm boundaries.

So now I was a hippie, and I guess I took it to the extreme, but come on—I had the hair! And yes, this is the part of the journey that may have contributed to the expansion of my numb spots.

Time passed, and at eighteen, I married. There was much more to my first husband, but in the end, our drug use and my fear of never truly being myself around him dissolved any chance for a real relationship. I had hit the brakes and drawn the line at heroin. Even my drug-addled mind knew that was very, very bad. After spending a couple of years in a drug-soaked fog, I sobered up on my own because I felt as if I was disappearing. In early January that year, I packed up my Volkswagen and drove home while singing along with "There Must Be Fifty Ways to Leave Your Lover" blaring on the radio.

It was a difficult landing at home with my parents. The primary reason for that was that we didn't tell my father the truth. He thought I was home because my husband and I were having a little trouble and I needed to get my head together. When he overheard me on the phone asking about renting an apartment, he blew a gasket. ("You're going to fuck up your marriage!") I hung up on the potential landlord and cried for the next twenty-four hours. I'd never heard him use that word before. So, I did what any moron would do. I moved into my Volkswagen Beetle. No worries; it was a Super Beetle. It wasn't long before I found a friend who let me stay at her house until I could find a place. Although it took me longer than it should have to forgive my dad. Poor guy. He never did get the full story.

Mom started out as a nurse's aide working for eighty-five cents an hour at a local hospital. She took classes, studied hard, and became an inhalation therapist, working nights. We talked a lot during the time after I left my first husband and before I married the second. One day, she shared her dream for me. "Honey, someday I hope you either get a job with an airline or with Baxter's." The actual name at the time was Baxter Travenol. They were a local medical products company that she knew of from her work at the hospital.

Eventually, she confessed that if she couldn't fly for free as an immediate family member, then helping to save lives was a darn good thing to do with my time while making money.

We figured I needed help to find a job, since I didn't have a lot of skills at this point, so I registered with an employment agency. I had waitressed, but that was really hard, and it didn't help me get rid of this feeling of disappearing; I really wanted that to go away. It took thirty days to get the one and only call I received from the agency. Baxter's was looking for a secretary. I'm telling you, my mom had some serious manifestation power! The agency gave me all kinds of tips to prepare for the interview and stressed the importance of not screwing things up for them. Baxter Travenol was their most important client.

I silently vowed to remember to get dressed for the interview and to avoid throwing up on anyone. Yes, my dreams had moved from forgetting to get dressed before going to school to forgetting to get dressed before going to work. Ah, the process of maturing. I got the job, got married again, and divorced within the first two years.

CHAPTER 2

Change Maker

When you change the way you look at things, the things you look at change.

—Dr. Wayne Dyer

I couldn't believe it. I was a senior program manager with more than thirty years at Baxter's, two degrees, and a certification in project management—and my management wouldn't listen to or even consider my recommendations.

That was the theme of my workdays during my last eighteen months of employment. In the preceding twenty-eight years or so, a lot had happened as I worked my way up the corporate ladder. My first degree, a BA "in marketing," took seventeen years to complete. I really wanted a BA in marketing, but the school didn't offer one, so they let me take all the classes they offered in marketing and called it a BA with a marketing concentration. All this took place while I was working in the R & D group for pharmaceuticals and medical products. My MBA took two years, and I started it the same month I completed the BA. That's because the company laid me off after twenty years, and I wanted to camouflage how recently I'd received my undergrad. Borrowing a phrase from an old friend, when it was all combined, it equaled a PhD from the School of Hard Knocks. I was hired back after a little over a year. Much of that time, I was a contractor working for the same company.

Once I joined the management ranks at work, people came to me, either for themselves or for their employees, for coaching. In some circles, it made me the go-to person for advice. It wasn't just individuals; I was also called upon to pull large-scale projects out of trouble and get them back on track. Sometimes it worked, and sometimes they were canceled based on the assessments and realistic time lines that we generated.

I had visions of how to make things better at an organizational level, but for some reason, in the later years, no one in management was interested in my ideas anymore. Those who worked for me and those who worked with me felt that what I had to offer the business was valuable. My closest friends at work told me, "You make so much sense; I don't know why management doesn't listen to you!" I was so frustrated, and I felt bad—really bad. For crying out loud! Was I disappearing again?

I decided to take advantage of the retirement program based on my first rule in life: *If it ain't no fun, don't do it.* (Note: My full list of rules is at the end of this book.) This job certainly was not fun anymore, nowhere near what it used to be. Of course, it's not so easy to walk away from a six-figure salary, but it was eating me alive. My brain was buzzing twenty-four hours a day, trying to figure out how to make it work—the right way. Somewhere along the line, I adopted this phrase into the rules I live by: "If you want something to change, change the way you look at it, or change what you're looking at." Of course, Dr. Wayne Dyer said it more eloquently.

I loved this new rule, and I used it whenever I could, usually during the coaching sessions that seemed to pop up all the time. It wasn't part of my job description, but it was something I really enjoyed. So many people are miserable at work for a variety of reasons: their boss, the work they do, the person next to them, or a fundamental disconnect with their values. Back then, and still today, when people come to me for advice, I suggest we start with exploring ways for them to see things differently. Just as an exercise, I ask them to think about the situation or the person from a different perspective, and together we explore scenarios around how they might change the way they look at the person or situation.

In cases where that approach doesn't work, we then explore how they might find something different to look at. Yep, that means, in most cases, getting a new job. Today, this exploration includes a discussion focused on what they would truly love to do. In the corporate setting, we are talking about Maslow's hierarchy, which tells us people long to make a difference. They long to be self-actualized—make a difference by making real contributions based on what they have to offer. And the best that they have to offer is directly linked to those things that they are truly passionate about.

We've all heard, "Do what you love, and you'll never work a day in your life." I enjoyed, and still enjoy, helping people define the things they love doing in their work. My approach to this was, and still is, to insist they move toward something. I let them know this: "If you are focused on just getting away, you don't need a coach. Coaching requires a destination involving your passions, your strengths, and those things you enjoy. You can use a coach for that." Having no destination is the direct route to repeating the same mistakes. My own memories of repeating mistakes include slapping my forehead while saying, "Oh no, not this again!"

So, there I was. Outside of coaching folks and working with the projects, I felt frustrated and angry, and I wondered once again if I was disappearing. I submitted my retirement papers and had at least six more months before I was free to run my own life!

I would become a consultant. People would hire me for my expertise, and I would be able to do the work that they weren't able to do themselves. As I thought about the differences between my current job and being a consultant, one thing became painfully obvious. I was so frustrated all the time. If I continued to show my frustration as a consultant, I wouldn't even make it through the initial interview. That realization led to the idea that I had to change immediately.

I decided to try looking at my job differently while I was preparing to look for something different. I created a new reality by playing. I would pretend that I would now be working with new clients for a management group that had just hired me as their new consultant. They needed me to produce outcomes based on what I could bring to the table to improve their business.

This change in perspective was one of the most pivotal points of my life. Of course, I didn't realize it then. Suddenly, I felt 100 percent better. All those things that used to drive me crazy were now opportunities for me to learn rather than to teach others to see it right (aka the way I saw things). I made a practice of carefully listening for their core needs, and I stopped worrying about terminology. I even felt compelled to listen to their suggestions. And darn it, there were several nuggets of information that I added to my consulting arsenal. I just needed to listen and be open to helping them, and I was helped in return! Who knew?

I worked on the projects and came back to "my client" with what he wanted. I would highlight the key things he'd asked for and then almost casually point out things I had added to facilitate the outcome he wanted. Since I was leaving, I no longer had my own agenda. I was just there to help make the projects successful. Okay, correction, I did have my own agenda—practice being a consultant—but that's all, honest!

I'd get a call with a request for action, and I'd listen carefully, take notes, and find myself saying, "Yes, we can make that work." This was a much different answer from my old standard. Before, I would explain to them what I thought they really meant. I corrected their terminology or rephrased the description of the outcome they were trying to convey. I now refer to this as my standard knucklehead response to a legitimate management request. My answer was anything but the magical words, "Yes, we can make that work."

Next thing I knew, I was hearing phrases from my boss like "Once again, Dee, you have exceeded my expectations!" Wow, this was amazing. I laughed out loud and thanked him. How many times had I counseled people to get themselves to a better place by changing how they looked at something? A lot, and yet it took me years to take my own counsel. I thought I was following my own advice by retiring, thinking that I was changing *what* I was looking at. Ah, but first I inadvertently changed *the way* I was looking at the situation. In retrospect, I was quitting corporate America to go into consulting … in corporate America. Not really changing up the *what* there.

Upon reflection, I didn't agree with the changes that were being made, and I felt what was happening was not right. I did not stop to think about what *right* actually meant. I had a vision in mind, and anything that deviated from my vision felt like a personal assault. I was helpless to the management changes in strategy and routine. I had some very good ideas, but what I didn't have were an open mind and open heart, because, once again, I felt as though I was disappearing, and I wasn't aware of the fact that I was making it happen myself! I fought the organizational changes by insisting, every time I could, on having things done the "right" way, which of course was my way.

It turned out that the right way was something so much larger than the way an organization was run. There are probably a thousand or more different right ways. I did find my right way after choosing to walk a painful and tedious path for a long time. Once I got to my true right way, it was so much easier. The right way for me was to be in service—to use my passions, expertise, and capabilities to serve the larger good.

In the corporate world, it was explained on meeting room posters: "Begin with the end in mind." It included getting to know the people around me, learning what their vision of the end product was, and finding a way to collaborate and contribute as much as I could by using my expertise and doing what I really enjoyed—getting things done. I stopped trying to revise the client's (or management's, in that case) vision.

Before this point, I was tripping over the details of *how* to get things done—the process. Once I focused on *what* was to be done, everything began to work. Once I stopped all that worry about disappearing, I stopped being offended while trying to achieve the *what*. I stepped out of the internal drama, and *wow,* I enjoyed my job again! Time flew by, and the joy I experienced in my work was wonderful once again.

It wasn't until I started looking into this information that I asked myself, "What changed here?" The answer popped up as I asked the question: I changed. I had never imagined the possibility of creating a scenario in my mind that would create an environment in which I could flourish. Let alone creating it all by myself despite the circumstances

13

surrounding me. Lacking that sort of imagination and believing that I was a victim of corporate changes resulted in an environment filled with everything I did not want.

I just couldn't see what I had been doing all along until I created the consulting environment, playing with the idea that I was working with my first client. In my mind, playing around, I created the place where I wanted to work. I did not like the answer when I asked, "Is it possible that I actually created that negative environment that surrounded me?"

Oh yeah, that's right. I created the exact thing I didn't want. Why? Because that was all I thought about. Constantly playing the soundtrack to my life: *Oh, this is wrong, this is wrong, wrong, wrong, and oh, and that's wrong too! The unfairness of these people—it's insulting!* Searching for the next wrong thing and the next, I watched and waited for the next person or event to show up and make me feel as if I was disappearing even more. Ha! Take a guess at who the only person in the entire universe was who could make me feel I was disappearing.

I had no idea that I was, am, and always shall be cocreating my life. I believed that what happened could actually "make me feel" a certain way, and I had no choice; it's the song of the victim. What the heck? "How did I become a victim of my own life? Oh, the horror! How can this be? I'm such a good person—so easygoing. I don't deserve this. *What?*"

That's how it was until the magical moment when I decided to change how I looked at my job, until I pretended that I was a consultant, that I was in my dream job and I was happy to help my new clients. I considered for a moment that this might be what it was like to be delusional, that I was employing some sort of escape mechanism to get me to my last day. But I didn't care. I was finally doing it. Why? Because my friend Carole would always tell me, "Act as though you are where you want to be, and you will get there." I love you, Carole White!

Carole and I worked in the lab together, along with some great people. Carole became my mentor because she would offer excellent alternative approaches to everyday events. I learned she had a strong spiritual background, had been a yoga instructor, and was a single mother of three children. Her wisdom throughout our careers enabled me to become more focused on my goals while maintaining a more spiritual approach. A unique approach in those days. The topics of corporate work and spiritual approaches were typically not part of the same conversations. Except with Carole.

When I changed my perspective to acting as though I was a consultant, everything else changed. Management was listening to my ideas, work was completed on time and on budget, plus I was receiving accolades. Management didn't know that I had changed the way I was thinking about my job. They were simply responding to me, and I suspect they were a bit relieved because I wasn't quite as, well, cynical.

Quick note: Did you know that up to 90 percent of your communication is in your body language and the tone of your voice? One could be saying something amazing, but if while doing it, one is sneering, eyerolling, or adding a little acid in the voice, no one listens. They are focused on one thing: "Run away!" What we feel is linked to what we think, and what we think comes through as tone, gestures, and body language. Even with the best poker faces, we all have tells; turns out I had screams.

So, how did I make the change? I can tell you it isn't a matter of flicking a switch. It took practice. And since I was there ten hours or more a day, I was able to practice a lot. The first step was to be vigilant to what the inside of me felt like. Was I relaxed and happy, or was I getting angry? There are physical sensations linked to our emotions, and we all have the ability to sense them. As it turned out, anger was, for me, the easiest sensation to feel. Perhaps that's because I spent several years angry at the world.

Now that I was on my way out, any time I went to a meeting, or the phone rang, or I was in a situation with management, I saw myself in a beautiful, natural place experiencing peace and joy. Yeah, I know it sounds weird, but honest, it works. After all, I really was right where I wanted to be—getting ready to go out and become the world's most amazing consultant. As interactions began with others, I worked hard to quit thinking and focused on listening. I would use those important consultant words, "So what I hear you saying ..." or "Can you say a little more about that?" I was even able to allow a brief silence after the person stopped talking. Just in case he or she had a little more information to share.

If I interrupted, I would excuse myself and ask the person to please finish what he or she was saying. If I started telling other people what they really meant, I would stop and make fun of myself by saying something like, "Oh, apparently I'm a psychic now. Maybe we should go back to you telling me what you mean."

And if all this wasn't enough, somewhere along the line before I retired, I was approached by three consulting firms and took a position with the company that was the best fit with what I was looking for! There I was—already living the life I had imagined. Wow!

On December 17 of that year, I officially retired from a job I enjoyed (again) and flew to Florida so my husband and I could board a cruise ship the next morning. Yep, that's right—Christmas on the high seas. Life was wonderful!

CHAPTER 3

Whoops!

I've looked at clouds from both sides now
From up and down and still somehow
It's clouds' illusions I recall

—Joni Mitchell

You are not the same as you were. You were much more ...
muchier; you've lost your muchness.

—The Mad Hatter in
Alice in Wonderland Jaded

A s a project manager, I guess I could have planned my departure a little bit better. It was pretty stressful between the emotional impact of actually leaving my job of thirty-plus years while packing and making final arrangements for my vacation cruise. After all those years at my job, the separation hit me hard, even if leaving was exactly what I wanted. I have vivid memories of hobbling onto the cruise ship thinking that no one else on earth needed a massage more than I did! That, and a good soak in salt water. My muscles were in knots, and my joints were all stiff. The cruise was just what I needed.

I retired on December 17, enjoyed a lovely cruise, and when I got back, went in for a mammogram. In mid-December, I had noticed a rather large lump in my left breast and assumed that a small coffee shop had moved in. They always caution us about drinking too much coffee before mammograms because it makes things a little lumpy. I'd been hitting the lattes hard and thought that I had a caffeine cyst. After all, I had just had a thorough exam in mid-November and all was well.

On January 12, I was diagnosed with an aggressive form of breast cancer. Whoops! Didn't see that coming!

I took the call from the doctor while in a craft store, supporting my cell phone with my left shoulder while looking at a lovely sky-blue sparkly flourish (that's a squiggly thing for you non-crafters). After the requisite pause to process the news, I calmly said, "Okay, what are the next steps?"

I immediately switched to professional project manager work mode. *Something went wrong. Let's define the work to be done and take the next steps.* The doctor and I briefly talked about the immediate next steps, and I ended the call, left the store, drove home, and told my husband.

"Well, I got the call. It's cancer. Oh, and I have to go grocery shopping."

"What? What the heck's wrong with you? You're going grocery shopping?" My husband was convinced I'd lost my mind.

He was acting like a normal person and expected me to do the same—be upset, for example, but I wasn't. I believe that the numb spots near my amygdala were partially why I was so calm and without fear. For the moment, I was processing the information, figuring out how to get used to the idea that I had cancer.

My plan, or better yet, my decision, was to research, assess, and of course, take action to get it resolved as soon as possible. I focused on taking action because this thing was obviously growing way too fast. I arranged for a surgical oncologist, and until I met with her, there really wasn't any more for me to do. I made sure my freak-out mechanism stayed in park for the time being because I knew that getting all crazy about this was the last thing my poor body needed.

The surgical oncologist described the cancer as a HER II positive, solid tumor, about the size of an egg (boiled, not fried). She said it was an aggressive type of cancer. No surprise there, since I noticed the lump within six weeks of my annual checkup. It was wild that it had come on like that, but I was now prepared to make things happen fast because if I waited too long, that thing would be the size of my head.

I thought a lot about the fact that my mother had had breast cancer. I learned that hers was different from what I had, and therefore, the treatment would also be very different. Hers was slow growing, and she must have had it for years by the time it was diagnosed as stage 4. But Mom got through it all, and she had been in her seventies. I was not that old. I'd be fine.

I truly believed that, because mine was brand spanking new and we were on top of it right away. Funny thing, by the way: when I had the mammogram done, the tumor didn't show up in imaging. It was huge and didn't show up. The technician found it as she was prepping me for the x-ray, but the x-ray looked great, a perfectly healthy breast. The doctor who read the x-ray and the technician's note about the large lump that was there despite what the image showed sent the letter recommending I go to the local breast cancer center to have an ultrasound. It showed up there, big time, and I was diagnosed from the biopsy taken that day.

I had a great team than included a surgical oncologist as well as an oncologist who managed the treatment plan and a doctor to oversee radiation. It was a standard protocol for a lumpectomy: two separate chemo treatments over twenty weeks; the surgery to remove the lump; and seven weeks of radiation treatments.

I have to say that during that first round of chemo, I did freak out a bit. When I finally lost it, it was because I thought that my husband hated me and wanted a divorce. I concluded this because he barely responded to me when I talked to him and was always so quiet and distracted. I was at the kitchen table one morning, newly bald and sporting quite the shine there in the sunlight, and asked him some silly, unimportant question. He didn't respond. He didn't even acknowledge that I'd spoken to him—again. I burst into tears and asked him through the sniffles and dribbles if he wanted a divorce. I could handle all this sick stuff, but I couldn't handle losing him. Well, he practically yelped out, "What? Are you crazy? What the hell are you talking about? Why would you even think that?"

Turns out that divorce wasn't on his mind at all; he was freaking out in his own way but trying not to upset me. Funny how those things happen. He didn't think it was so funny, but looking back, I can't help but chuckle a bit. Not only was I seriously ill, but yikes, I was now there, twenty-four hours a day! He was semi-retired, driving a school bus on a split shift, and had been having the house to himself most of the day for years. His whole routine had been just chucked out the window. ("Honey, hope you enjoyed the cruise because now I'm home twenty-four/seven, in your face with cancer—ta da!")

I think at first, he was wondering how long I would be around. He was really concerned that I might die. As for me, I didn't give more than a few minutes to the idea of death. No worries there. We would kick this thing. Mom had done it with the cards stacked against her and some archaic treatments; I would do just fine. I believed this at my core. I wasn't trying to believe something, or repeating affirmations to change what I was really thinking. I just believed it and didn't doubt it. And I didn't think about thinking about it; I just moved forward. I simply knew what I knew.

In my earlier years at Baxter as a lab technician, I worked on a disposal medical device that delivered chemotherapy. That experience helped me grasp what was happening now. Any time I thought about working on that chemotherapy delivery device, or caring for my mom during her struggle, I heard the lyrics "I've looked at clouds from both sides now, from up and down, and still somehow …"

I was simply determined to face it all head on. For example, when I found out that I would definitely lose my hair because of the type of chemo I would be taking, I decided to shave my head. From my research, I knew that hair loss was one of the biggest concerns for people going through chemo. To me, the horror was more about having clumps of hair fall out and sporting random bald spots looking like some sort of apocalyptic zombie. Well, "it is what it is," so I decided to ask my beautician, Beckie, to shave my head. I, of course, needed to exploit the opportunity to play with it, so I asked her to first give me a Mohawk. I have to say, I looked pretty cool. I've got pictures.

After that, I went wig shopping with my trusted friend Sue and had some real fun with that. I took some great shots with all sorts of wigs. It was like a model photo shoot. My favorite was the Auntie GaGa shot where I put on a bright blond straight wig, very different from my curly brown hair. I uploaded all the shots to the blog I was writing to keep friends and family up to date on what was happening and how I was doing. I enjoyed writing the blog and was so grateful that I didn't have to repeat the news over and over.

I learned that the well-meaning concerns of so many people who were curious to know what was happening could have easily resulted in my living inside the cancer every day by talking about it over and over. My friend Dorothy was the one who told me about the blog site that spared me from constantly repeating the same information. This way I could report all the updates on treatments and how I was feeling whenever I wanted to and do it just once. This was great because the larger the friends-and-family circle, the more repetition. God bless the blog!

After the second dose of chemotherapy, I removed the remaining stubs of gray hair by gently rubbing my head over a large paper plate. I was mesmerized by this because my tiny gray hairs sparkled a little bit and looked like falling snow. (If you're asking yourself where the brown hair went, it was on Becky's floor. I'm talking about those infamous roots that grew out in the meantime.) I was surprised, however, at how sore my scalp was; even though the tiny hairs fell out easily, the skin was not happy to let go. Once my scalp could shine without the interruption of the stubble, it was much more comfortable.

On the bright side of the darkness, it turned out that I had won the health care lottery. Within the last two years or so, they had completed clinical trials on an amazing biotech drug called Herceptin. That drug was specifically designed to target and kill my kind of tumor. The fact that the tumor was so aggressive also made it quite vulnerable to chemotherapy. We shrank it with some serious chemo and then brought in the Herceptin. Twenty-three weeks later, they plucked that shriveling tumor right out, along with a couple of lymph nodes. Right there, during surgery, they checked the lymph nodes and declared that the cancer hadn't spread. Once I healed up a bit, we followed up with seven weeks of radiation, just to make sure. Not fun, and not easy. However, it worked, and I'm here to tell the story.

I didn't tell everyone what I was going through then because I realized that when I told some people they would break in half at the news. Their pain was real and palpable and rested directly on top of my own. It happened when I told the first person or two, and then I just couldn't do it anymore. As a result, there were a few people that I didn't tell until after treatment was complete. Frankly, I think they're still a little peeved at me, but hey—I had the cancer and was therefore promoted to spoiled rotten princess who could do whatever the heck she wanted to do!

Everyone was so kind and always asked what they could for me; they sincerely wanted to know how they could help. My response was simple. I told them that the best thing they could do for me was to make me laugh. I loved all the emails and cards, funny stories, jokes, and pictures people sent to me. And I laughed and laughed.

Chemo started in February, surgery happened in July, and radiation ended in September. I began Herceptin infusions near the end of March and continued until March 1 of the following year. After being diagnosed and submerged in the treatment, I had a lot of time to think about putting myself first, and to do some things for myself simply because I wanted to.

First, I focused on applying the things I had learned from my mentor, Carole. More on her in a minute. Right out of the gate, I was compelled to have the right imagery around me and asked my husband to print out pictures of Roy Rogers and Mother Theresa. Weird, huh? He thought so too. Then I bought a bumblebee pillow to rest my feet on while typing because the wood floor in my office/craft room was so cold. Yes, I had two pairs of slippers and was just too lazy to go get them every time I sat at my computer on the other side of the house. Besides, I needed a bumblebee.

I had so much time on my hands, and I thought about all the information I had learned over the years about visualization. *Focus on what you want, not on what you don't want. Begin with the end in mind.* (Thank you, Stephen Covey.) I had heard of people imagining magical birds pecking away the tumors and all sorts of other self-healing techniques. I was inspired to do my part for my own healing through visualization and having conversations with my cells.

During those first twenty years at the company, when I worked on that chemotherapy delivery device, I was blessed to make a wonderful friend named Carole. She became my mentor. She taught me so many wonderful concepts around so many mysteries involving the powers of my own mind and attitude. "Act as though" was an important one—acting as though I was already the person I wanted to be, doing whatever it was I wanted to do. She told me to believe it and be grateful for it.

Carole said, "Visualize who you are, what you're doing, how you dress, where your office is, every detail." The visualization strategy that she taught me worked well in building my career. I had to take a few steps on my own to help it along, to show the universe I was serious.

Now I had to apply this to my diagnosis. It had worked for me in my career development efforts, so I envisioned myself in excellent health. I saw myself hiking, dancing, laughing, traveling, consulting, and working with amazing people. I even tried visualizing doing cartwheels again. Even with a deep sense of commitment to the process, I couldn't quite pull that one off. I just couldn't completely believe it at my core, but the image of it absolutely fulfilled my need to laugh. Being able to laugh at myself is truly one of the greatest gifts I have.

Carole taught me a lot and validated so much of what I believed in my heart but had a hard time articulating. I wasn't a religious person, but I had my own perspective on how this miraculous universe worked. For one thing, it didn't involve a white-haired guy with a beard, sitting on a throne deciding everything for everyone and doling out blessings and punishments as necessary. It had to be so much more than that. Why go through the work of creating these infinite universal miracles, including the entire human race, only to throw a rather large section of it into a fiery hell pit? I was confused and angry about that whole concept. My discussions with the lovely Carole, along with the seminars and lectures we attended, helped me to build a solid spiritual foundation. This foundation gave me the ability to fly to the highest heights of imagination while standing strong in my beliefs. Thank you, Carole. I love you! And thank you, universe, for Carole!

Why Roy Rogers? Well, he saved my life countless times from a myriad of scary situations that little girls make up, in the dark, before drifting off to sleep. He saved me from monsters, bad guys, and yes, even some serious illnesses. He had, after all, magical powers! He would show up and—ta da!—I was safe and life was wonderful, so sleep came easily.

Mother Theresa had a big impact on me. When cancer comes for a visit, the word *fight* comes up in a lot of different ways. "Wage war, fight like a girl, and beat it back!" I knew immediately that I could not wage war on something that didn't sleep while taking up residence in my body. Me, I had to sleep, so I needed another strategy. As soon as I thought that, inspiration arrived in the form of a quote from

Mother Theresa. I still don't know when or where I first saw it, and I don't remember the exact words, but I remembered it this way: When Mother Theresa was asked to join a march against the Vietnam War, she declined. But she told them that if they ever planned to march for peace, just to let her know and she'd be there.

That was it! I was marching for health; I was all about healing and health. No war, no anger, no bitter fight, just a peaceful march for health. I wasn't marching alone, either. I began to regularly talk to all that made up my body. I started with an apology for not taking better care of all of them, and promised I'd do better as we moved forward. But for now, I asked everyone (cells, atoms, particles, and the spaces between) to please shun the cancer. I told them, "No fighting, no biting, kicking, or scratching. Just turn your back. Give no nourishment, no attention, no aid. Each of you, focus on perfect health and march on toward that state of being. I will handle all communications with the uninvited guest."

I said to the cancer, "Hello, cancer, I see you and feel you. Thank you for stopping by to remind me of so many important things. However, your work here is done now. I have received the message loud and clear. You are not welcome here. You do not belong here, and no one here will help you. You are gone; you are done; you are over. The decision is final, and now time only needs to pass." I saw the tumor shriveling from sheer lack of nourishment and loneliness.

I addressed my body repeatedly, reminding my cells to march for health, let the chemo do its thing, and rejuvenate with joy as we arrived at perfect health. I called one of the more severe drugs "Lady A" for Adriamycin. She was a tough one; she took my hair and kicked my butt, but I welcomed her with open arms and thanked her for kicking the crap out of that tumor.

Then there's that toasty-warm bumblebee pillow. I love the image of the bumblebee. A friend of mine from many years ago used to sell cosmetics. She had a gold bumblebee brooch that she won for meeting a sales quota. I thought it was odd, but she told me that if man were to design a bumblebee today, it would look much different because, according to our understanding of the physics of flight, the bumblebee shouldn't be able to fly. The body is too big, and the wings are too small. Well, no one told the bumblebee that, thank goodness. The image of a bumblebee gives me comfort in knowing that no matter what, I can do it. It is the echo of proof relating to what my mother told me a million times while I was growing up: "You can do anything you set your mind to!"

These ideas and the imagery I selected to remind myself of my accountability to my own health meant everything to me; they still do. This was by no means a picnic, but I know that my attitude throughout the journey and my clear vision of health made it easier than it might have been. I responded to the situation with the healthiest possible vision and created an entirely new interaction with my body in order to move back to a state of health.

There is another important element to this story that happened while I was sitting in my recliner chair petting my cat. This was my "go to" position during treatment. It frequently included mint chocolate chip ice cream (for medicinal purposes, of course). My cat appeared not to care about the occasional green droplets of ice cream on his fur. He cleared them away with aplomb. He was such a good boy!

Anyway, the important element came to me one day: I have always wanted to be a motivational speaker. With so much to do and so much going on, I hadn't thought about that for quite a while—for years—but it popped in during this thinking session. As I mentioned, thinking became a full-time job for me for a while. I loved helping people connect to one another or to the right job, or just connect their own dots to find their own brand of joy. I had always imagined that when I became a consultant, my mission would be to help people get things done *and* find their joy.

Now that I had gotten through the "Oh, crap; I have cancer" phase and was dealing with it, I realized that it was true: we really needed to be careful what we wished for. One problem with my vision was that I had never felt that I had a good enough story to be a motivational speaker. For one thing, I never considered ever sharing the information I did in chapter 1 about my "sordid past." There were a couple of lessons there around what I thought about my life and the types of constraints I put on myself with that line of thinking. So, my speaking engagements on project management were as motivational as they could be on one level, but I always wished I could go a little deeper.

I chuckled at that particular yearning while nibbling on my mint chocolate chip ice cream. I thought, *Well, this Roy Rogers, Mother Theresa, and bumblebee combo helping me to march for health through this breast cancer thing is quite the jewel. Now, there's a motivator that can go deep! Heck, I can write a book someday!* And I laughed about that old saying, "Be careful what you wish for."

I laughed at myself, I laughed at the irony, and I laughed at everything. Since I had become a nearly full-time thinking person, I laughed at all the wonderful inspiration that was coming my way without even trying! I honestly hadn't shared this part of my journey with anyone other than my husband for fear of … I don't know … pity, I guess. But at this point, it was very funny to me. And then I slept. I moved through it all and tucked my dream of becoming a motivational speaker away, but not too deeply because whenever I looked at the idea of it, I have to say it was sort of sparkly and filled with light. I liked it.

Fast forward to the following year. I was done with everything cancer and chemo and had quite the cute spikey hairdo. The short spikey cut was a huge change for me, having held on to the remnants of the wild hippie hairdo of the seventies. I was now consulting, and everything was going very well. And there, in the back of my mind was another darn song: "Is that all there is? Is that all there is? Is that all there is to life? Then let's keep dancing ..."

While this was playing in the back of my mind, two people I love very much said to me on separate occasions, "Dee, you've lost your hippie." I don't think that either one of them realized just how deeply that hurt me.

I was still a hippie. I loved tie-dye and fringe, and although I held down a corporate management job, I didn't sell out ... completely. I am literally Bohemian, for crying out loud! This was an insult! Me, *not a hippie?* Was it because I had lost the hairdo? I was melancholy, deflated, and disappearing again, not because of the hippie remarks but because I feared the life I was living at that moment might really be all there was. I kept thinking that I should be doing something. I had so much more to give, and I was just stirring around in the dust of my own life. Really, was that really all there was ... really?

Shortly thereafter, my husband and I were watching the latest version of *Alice in Wonderland, Jaded,* where she goes back to Wonderland as an adult. Somewhere in there, the Mad Hatter said, "Alice, you've lost your muchness!" I knew right then and there that that was what was wrong with me. I had lost my muchness! Something much more tangible than my hippie! And I wept.

CHAPTER 4

On the Other Side

Is that all there is, is that all there is?
If that's all there is, my friends, then let's keep dancing
Let's break out the booze and have a ball
If that's all there is

—Sung by Peggy Lee;
Written by Jerry Leiber and Mike Stoller

In December of the year of treatment, I was blessed to find the Unity Spiritual Center close to my home. I had heard about Unity from my mentor, Carole, and would periodically search the Internet hoping to find one nearby. Well, there it was. One had just moved into the neighboring town, so my husband and I began services there the following February.

During one of those first Sunday mornings as the service started, I was wondering if this was what depression was—losing my muchness? Was I depressed, or was I melancholy? How the heck did this happen, getting through all that, only to live my life according to that "Is That All There Is?" song?

Then, in the background, I heard the reverend say, "Do you feel like you should be doing something more with your life, but you just don't know how to make it happen?"

I very nearly jumped up and screamed, "Hallelujah, Reverend Tom!" Well, this wasn't that sort of church, but I do believe that the people would have been okay with it if I had. Instead, I realized that he was talking about a class. I told my husband that I was going attend that class. It was a ten-week seminar guiding attendees in defining and achieving their dreams. I loved it!

The class involved video during class time, as well as discussion, in addition to the CDs and workbook that we completed each week. It was all about prosperity of the spirit, and it taught me how much my thoughts carved out the life I was leading.

I learned so much from that class, and I wanted more. I attended the certification seminar in LA. After that, I researched even more. And I am researching still. I do this because I love this stuff! I'm hearing the same messages now from a variety of sources. It's not any one person's material but many voices relaying the messages of so many other people's material. I hear it in church, on CNN, in business, in music—it's everywhere. We create our own limitations.

This information has been around for centuries and has been taught in so many ways. Once I found it, soaked it in, and worked at applying it, everything changed. For me, it was the key to living the life I loved to live, using my passions while being free to do what I wanted to do, with purpose. Why, oh why, wasn't this taught in school?

Back to the class at my church. The first question I had to answer was "What is the life you would truly love to live?" We were supposed to approach it using a magic wand that allowed us to do anything, go anywhere, and have everything we ever wanted. What did that look like? I blushed, a kind of pink with purple highlights. I bounced the imaginary magic wand on my forehead for a while, thinking very carefully. Finally, I tossed my pen/magic wand and was just plain embarrassed because I didn't have a clue what my perfect life would look like. Well, no wonder I was feeling so down. I couldn't even imagine something wonderful. Imagining was playing with the mind. I could do that. I was born to play, for crying out loud! I coached people all the time on finding their joy. I should have had this all figured out. Well, it turned out everyone else in the class was in the same boat. Phew! That was some relief, but come on; it was time to just belly up to the table and take a double dose of my own medicine. And then something happened. I felt the freedom to explore; it was as if rusty old chains were dropping off of me, and I could hear them hit the floor.

As it turned out, the fact was that we were all in the same boat. That was a common thread running through the material. This boat, however, was the universe. We are all in it, of it, connected to and by it. The universe was also called God or the Creator. You may have another name for it, but you get the gist. The universal energy.

I hadn't thought of it that way before, but it made more sense to me than I can tell you. It was a tuning fork going off in my head. I was so grateful for the introduction to the material, but I couldn't be tied to one message source on this. I needed more, and as I opened to the possibilities, I found it everywhere. It was like deciding to buy a brand-new car, say a blue Ford. One reason I liked it was because of its unique color of blue. Shortly after the purchase, I see blue Fords everywhere, and maybe even similar shaped cars from other makers. They are everywhere around me, but I didn't notice them before. I wasn't open to the idea of a blue Ford—not because I didn't believe in them or because I didn't like them, but because it just never dawned on me to think about the existence of a blue Ford. And then, all life converged on the head of a pin. That blue color was *so* beautiful. Then I see it in clothing and dishware. There is even a brand of chewing gum with the same color wrapper. Really, this was how it happened. Everything was everywhere, but I only saw it when I directed my attention to it. Funny, huh?

If I'm walking through the halls of my business clients, I can see the connection to this material in those posters or even guidance documents advising us to "Begin with the end in mind!" Define the requirements up front. Henry Ford himself must have been quoted eight billion times: "If you think you can do a thing, or if you think you can't do a thing, *you're right.*" It's a great quote, and we'll explore it further a little later in the book.

Dale Carnegie, author of *How to Win Friends and Influence People,* urged Napoleon Hill, author of *Think and Grow Rich,* to research and write about what successful businesspeople have in common. It's the same thing successful athletes and many spiritual people have: perspective. There are a lot of successful people who subscribe to these ideas. But a great way to understand success is to look at the word *failure.*

Some people take a risk and fail once, twice, or even three times. That's where the sorting begins. At this point, or prior to this point, some people quit. Two or three failures are proof positive that they were really bad at whatever it was they were trying. A business venture, relationships, publishing a book, losing weight, knitting, painting—the list is pretty much endless. "Oh, I tried that a couple of times. I sucked at it, so I gave it up."

Thomas Edison described failure as feedback, nothing more. When one thing didn't work, he tried something else. All successful businesspeople have stories of what some would call failure, but for them it was information, feedback from experimentation; I like to think of it as play.

When I hear the phrase "Perspective is everything," it makes me think of my marketing classes. The customers' perspective of our product or business is the only thing that counts. Even if they are dead wrong about us, it doesn't matter because they won't be back. Their misguided opinion of our product is something they believe, and since that is what they believe, that is their reality. They're gone.

Ever find yourself in a conversation about political figures with someone from the opposing side? Sometimes the discussion escalates to a debate and then to a fight. You walk away, shaking your head. *What the heck is wrong with her? How can she be so blind to the truth? She is an otherwise intelligent person, but on this topic, she's an idiot!*

You are absolutely grounded in your belief, and the idea that there can be anything of value, even in a point of view that you believe is worthless, is simply not on your radar. When you believe, truly believe, something so completely, there are simply no other possibilities. It's carved in stone, granite; it's final.

Well, I'm here to tell you, maybe not so much. Our beliefs are so absolute for one reason and one reason only. They are what we believe. In reality, the possibilities are endless. Your belief is first and foremost a thought that you have on a topic, any topic. It becomes something that you believe. It is quite likely that we all have beliefs that we will never change for the simple reason that we know them to be facts, but it would be a lot of fun to find some of your less-than-foundational beliefs to play with during this book. Maybe something like a belief that you can't find a better job, can't lose weight, can't write a book, can't pull together an extra hundred dollars to buy that something special, can't get comfortable with your body image. It helps if it is something that you believe but wish you didn't. Think about it for a bit; think of something, and when you're ready, come out and play.

CHAPTER 5

The Universal Truth

Nothing can stop the man with the right mental attitude from achieving his goal; nothing on earth can help the man with the wrong mental attitude.

—Thomas Jefferson

I shall call God working in our lives "Law." … Then as we strive to work with the Law, we are living closer to God, and such living brings better understanding.

—Raymond Holliwell, *Working with the Law*

I love the thought of infinite, universal possibilities and the amazing lives we live through the blessings of this splendid and mysterious universe. I love contemplating the spiritual connections to everything and feeling grateful. Grateful for color and wind, toes and antennae—oh, and feathers! I'm grateful for family and friends, oceans and mountains, breath, clouds, and the ability to keep coming up with more items on this list every day. I am grateful for dark chocolate and free will, and of course, mint chocolate chip ice cream.

I'm also in love with science. It's not a close relationship. After all, my degrees are focused on marketing and business. But I've been around engineers and scientists most of my career and wouldn't have it any other way. (Okay, there you go; I'm grateful for engineers and scientists.) There is something mesmerizing as I learn how things work, like getting a peek behind the curtain. For example, I used elevators every day at my job and didn't know how they worked. Occasionally, I imagined the tremendous amount of moving parts and electronics it took to create it and wondered, just how did the human mind figure all that out? While working with the scientists who had dedicated their lives to bringing medicines to the market, I would hear them talk to one another, and for a little while, I would be able to keep up until they went in deep. I marveled at the capacity of the human brain and stood in awe of what they knew about the liquids we packaged in bags to help patients recover. They used words I couldn't even pronounce, and sometimes there would be an "Aha!" I loved those times because I knew a solution to the problem was on the way.

I loved hearing about how the body worked, or the solar system, and I had a real soft spot in my heart for the industrial-size automated equipment that I saw in the manufacturing plants. An entire room was filled with machinery; at one end, bits and pieces were put into the massive equipment, and when it was running, the floor shook just a little. Then medical products dropped out of the other end, perfectly coiled, capped off, and packaged!

So, how do all the mysteries of the universe come together? I found it in a book called *Working with the Law* by Raymond Holliwell. I use some of his work as a foundation for the information I share through coaching, writing, and speaking.

Real prosperity is in our relationships with everyone around us—having loving, trusting, and occasionally hysterically funny conversations with family, friends, coworkers, the cashier, the taxi driver, and the people on the street. Relating to other people in a way that is a blessing to all is a valid measure of prosperity.

It's about how we earn our living in a way that enriches us. It applies to our health, where we can be healthy, well, and whole no matter the circumstances. For example, even with cancer, I found so much to be grateful for when it came to good health. Everything else was working. My biological machinery was affected in a couple of places by the treatments, but my amazing system would recuperate, and in the meantime, I could get to the freezer for some delicious mint chocolate chip ice cream, which penetrated any temporary barriers that the chemo might have put up around my precious little taste buds. My heart pumped, my legs walked, and I could talk for hours, read, comprehend, and write. Even at my worst, a whole lot was going well with this ole biological carrying case.

I was able to focus on what was working. You see, everything begins with a thought, including our beliefs. Our thoughts and beliefs are signals to the universe. They are tendrils sharing our desires, expectations, and intentions. The signals require a certain emotional intensity associated with them. That's the juice. It doesn't really matter whether it is overwhelming gratitude for what we have or overwhelming despair over what we don't have; over time, juice is juice. Again, our thoughts become beliefs and our beliefs become facts of our lives.

Let's bring it in a little closer now. The universe is, of course, everywhere. It includes the space between the particles that make up absolutely everything. Each of us has a spark within us, a spark that is the soul, the higher self, the observer. Call it what you will, but it's there in

39

every single person and is the mechanism of our connection to source, the universal, infinite, and ever-expanding possibilities. We can open up to it or pinch it off through our own free will.

If your self-esteem is low and you believe that you are less than other people, or that you're stupid or fat or unworthy of all the splendor the universe has to offer, you're not just speaking of yourself. You're including all that dwells within you—your body, your mind, your soul, the particles that are you, and the spaces between. You include that which creates everything that is you. These particles and cells, and the spaces between, by the way, are just a few of the places where the universe dwells. So, when you're finding fault, be clear with whom you are finding fault! Is critiquing the perfection of the universe what you want to be doing? I don't think you can separate yourself from your creator.

Perhaps you might choose to give an enriched and expansive life a shot. Try bringing joy into your life and changing the negative thoughts about yourself, and bring joy to those around you by using the same tools you've been using to find fault with the handiwork of the universe (i.e., you). If it helps, go ahead; click your heels three times. Just sayin'.

CHAPTER 6

Meet the Observer

People's minds are changed through observation and not through argument.

—Will Rogers

You can observe a lot by watching.

—Yogi Berra

I was saying earlier that it's really strange—you can almost step outside yourself and observe yourself running, and that's what I was doing.

—Marcus Allen

Have you ever experienced seeing something so frivolous and feeling that you just had to have it because it was so clever or cute or just so darn cool? Even though you had no use for it, you still bought it.

There is a conversation going on in your head saying something like this:

"*Oh*, look at that! It's *so* cool! I have to have it!"

"Don't be an idiot. You're wasting your money."

Then that second voice reprimands you the all the way home—and maybe even every time you look at the object, because of course, you did make the purchase.

That is a conversation between two voices. There is a third presence in this vignette, which we'll call *the observer*. You can tell who the observer is by what the observer does not do. It does not wish for anything; it does not berate you; it does not talk down to you. The observer observes and occasionally may make a suggestion, quietly, softly, but it mostly observes.

If you are aware, you can find the observer during the above internal debate. It is in the background and observes that you are struggling with a purchasing decision and now you are berating yourself. It observes. It's a witness; it sees and does not judge. It's the one who sees what is happening inside your head but isn't a part of the fracas. The very second you recognize that you're having a conversation in your head over a purchasing decision, that is the insight of the observer. The very second you realize you're observing this conversation and the observer, and you question whether you've lost your mind, you've booted the observer out and moved to the second, and frequently mean, voice.

The ability to observe without judgment or emotion, to me, is part of your highest self; it knows and accepts everything about you with love. No judgment; only acknowledgment of what exists at the moment. It is the source of that gentle, tiny voice that leaves you with the feeling that you should bring the umbrella as you're leaving the house on a sunny day. It is always there, lovingly observing, but we don't always realize it because of all the incessant babbling going on in there. We have such a cacophony of thoughts competing with each other that the possibility of actually having an observer isn't imagined, acknowledged, or recognized; nor can it be heard.

So much of our thinking space is taken up with the same thoughts we had yesterday and the day before. Somewhere on the negative side of the energy spectrum one can hear, *I hate myself. I'm fat. I'm ugly. No one likes me. I'm so stupid; I can't get anything right. Look at those dishes piling up; I'm so lazy. Oh boy, there I go again!*

And as we go deeper into the negative energy side, we may choose to replay all the old videos of all the worst things that have ever happened to us, the worst things we've done, our mistakes, our downfalls, our failures, and our most embarrassing moments. Over and over, around and around, like a hamster on a wheel.

The goal is to move along the spectrum and head out of the negative energy side and over to the positive side. I think that most of us are living near the middle, skewed to one side or the other. Those who are deeply and chronically depressed dwell a little further away. If that describes you, please seek treatment. I am not a therapist; I'm a coach. I coach people to recognize the possibilities for the sole purpose of moving forward in their lives. All this takes practice and patience. None of this is cause for finding flaws with yourself. It's new. Like learning to ride a bike or play the piano, or even like a child learning to walk. Practice; trial and error; fall and get up again, again, and again. It isn't like a light switch that you can just "clap on."

In order to get to know your observer, start by acknowledging that it is there. I think of it as the third level. For me, I can be thinking about one thing, but in the background, there can be something else going on—a grocery list, a sense of having to hurry and get to something else, or the faulty plotline of the movie I saw the night before.

I'm not kidding here. First, you have to know that the panicky voice whining for that second piece of cake or that cleverly designed thingamabob is not the observer. The voice that calls you an idiot or fat is, again, not the observer. The observer is quiet, loving, and always there.

Let's meet mine as an example. I'm sitting here, right now, writing this and loving it. While I'm typing, I'm thinking about what comes next, I'm feeling very grateful, and I want more coffee. I stop to drink the coffee, again loving that I am working on this book, and then, as I hold the cup and think all these thoughts, I leave the words behind. Then I can feel a presence partially in me but seeing things from an angle, as though it is slightly above or beside me. It sees what I'm doing and hears what I'm thinking. Since my observer is playing a key role in what is going on right now, I have to mention that there are a whole bunch of typos that I now have to go back and fix. Once I hit that third level of awareness, the first level, where things are physically going on, gets a little fuzzy. Now if you're intrigued and want more, we're going to have to mention the big *M*.

Yeah, that's right, meditation. I know—I can hear you: "I can't mediate. I've tried it, and I can't do it." My advice to you right now is to shut up. I say it with a loving and respectful tone, but shut up. Stop saying that. As long as you say, "I can't," you are right. Even though you are meditating when you say that, you're having a negative meditation experience that is being crafted to ensure you never meditate again.

Remember, in this life, you're in charge. It's your show. Your observer and the universe aren't going to tell you what to do. It is your job to live this life and provide experiences with the observer and the universe as part of an infinitely expanding life force. Whatever you experience, the universe experiences, and as a result, everything grows. Our individual experiences and all the consequences are part of the universal stew. Our free will determines the lives we lead. That means we have oh-so-much more choice than we ever realized. And getting to know our personal observer is an important step in finding our joy. It's a change from trying to make things happen to just letting them happen. It's time to give the cacophony a rest.

If you like puzzles, for example, while playing with one, you might find yourself working on it for much longer than you planned. When you finally get up to stretch, you see that two hours flew by in what seemed like twenty minutes. Einstein calls that the relativity of time. That was a meditation. Your thoughts quieted, and you were focused. It can happen while doing anything that can take you to a calm place where you are unaware of most everything except the task at hand. That's the proof that you can mediate.

A couple of things to know. You will always have thoughts. Like those moving ticker tape–like banners you see flashing across the bottom of the screen while watching the news. They show stock prices or more news while the newscaster is talking about a different news story. They are there, steadily flowing across the screen. Sometimes I try to listen to the newscaster, read the banners, and drink coffee.

Other times, you focus on what is being said because it's caught your attention. You focus and don't see anything else, including the fact that the cat is now drinking your coffee. (Too much cream is my guess.)

Pick a word for the sole purpose of catching your focus on something. Popular words are *love*, *peace*, and *honor*. I'm telling you here and now you can also choose words like *shoe, wall, door,* or *ice cream.* Okay, I can't use *ice cream,* as you know, because I move into some sort of mint chocolate chip delirium. Back to you. Pick something you can use as focal point. Another method is to focus on your breath. For me, that involves two words: *inhale* and *exhale.* (Yes, correlate them to the appropriate activity.)

Let's run an experiment in relaxation. We're not meditating yet. This is for the purpose of intentionally relaxing. Think about your neck and shoulders. Lean back, focus on relaxing them, and don't stop until you feel them relax. They should be dropping a little bit, but mostly, you should be able to feel them relax and kind of expand a bit. Experiment with this instead of trying to learn to relax and meditate all at once. Lean back. Continue to let go of those shoulders and see if you move it down your back, really feeling it. Try it with a couple of other areas: arms, legs, hips, anything you like.

When you sit down to meditate, you will send relaxation feelings down your body in a warm cascade from your head to your toes. If it feels as if something won't relax, leave it alone and be more relaxed in general. By that, I mean more relaxed than you were before you sat down. Find perfection in what you have, not in some false ideal of relaxation.

Your mind will wander. That is perfect and beautiful. Bring it back to your focal point. I once read a couple of things written by a Zen monk who wrote about the fact that we all have monkey minds; the monkeys run around wild in there sometimes. Meditation is the act of calming them, and the way to handle your mind when it wanders it to treat it as you would a beloved toddler who is going off track a little bit. Gently guide that toddler back kindly and lovingly. That way, you move your mind from a wild monkey to a sweet, curious toddler who needs a little guidance once in a while. Try not to beat it up for that. It kills the mood.

Begin with a five-minute commitment. Begin the process by getting comfortable in a chair. Stay away from the bed. Falling asleep is one of the big distractions. I believe it was Deepak Chopra who answered the question, "What does it mean when I fall asleep while meditating?" He said, "It means you need sleep."

I recently heard him say we should all mediate once a day. He acknowledged that there are some who say they don't have time to meditate. For them, he suggested meditating twice a day.

Okay, this is enough to get you started. Give it a shot. Relax, focus on one thing, and be gentle and loving with your monkey mind. If you just relax, stop judging, and stop trying so hard, you will have a couple of moments with your observer.

CHAPTER 7

The Declaration Is Independence

We hold these truths to be self-evident: that all men are created equal; that they are endowed by their Creator with certain unalienable rights; that among these are life, liberty, and the pursuit of happiness.

—Thomas Jefferson

Are you dependent on another person? I mean, are you completely dependent on someone to give you permission or approval to live your life completely and fully? Do you believe that you simply cannot make decisions on what you want or need without consulting and gaining the approval of someone else? Are there circumstances that you feel dictate what you can and cannot do, such as a lack or money of education, or feeling you are too old or too young? Are you feeling trapped where you are and helpless to do anything about it because you believe that there isn't anyone to pull you out?

If this is true, then you do not have a sense of your own essential freedom. It is an awareness that all of us should have, but many of us don't. It can be pinched off at an early age because of how you process early childhood experiences. These experiences can range from absolute horrors to consistently hurt feelings because someone important wasn't there for you. In addition, sometimes older people fall into the dependence hole because they tried to go after something (person, job, hobby) and it didn't work out, and they wind up trapped in the idea that they are now, and always will be, a failure because they believe that there isn't anyone to pull them out.

And the root cause is—the belief. We all have thoughts, billions of them, but perhaps in reality it's hundreds because we all rerun the thoughts we had yesterday, this morning, and five minutes ago. Over and over in our heads, the thoughts flow by, and we get hold of some of those thoughts and convert them into beliefs—full-on, top-to-bottom, no-way-around-it beliefs.

Once we convert thoughts into beliefs, we have a sense that they are completely and undeniably true facts. They are absolutes. Anyone who doesn't see it our way is flawed in some manner; they don't understand because they haven't been through what we've been through, so how could they know? Well, there are people out there right now who have been through what you have been through—some experienced much worse events—and they did go through it. Some of them become missionaries, letting others know that it is possible to get through it, and they share their experiences. How did they get through it? Is it because fundamentally they're better than you, stronger, luckier?

No. When they thought about overcoming it, they attached themselves to thoughts of getting through it and converted them to beliefs. What you believe about your life becomes your life. If at this moment you are thinking thoughts to defend your belief, please take a moment to think, *What if there is another way? What if I've convinced myself of something, and what if I can try it again, only with a more appealing outcome? What if I gave that a shot?* It's an exercise in thinking and asking larger questions. What if you just experiment with it on your own, without the approval of anyone—just decide to give it a go and see what happens?

Many of our beliefs are inherited from our families and friends. We learn them at an early age, and we are bound to them. We are bound to them because we believe we are bound to them, which, of course, binds us to them. Inventory your beliefs and determine whether they represent what you want in life.

I first discovered this when I read Viktor Frankl's book *Man's Search for Meaning*. He was a psychiatrist as well as a survivor of Auschwitz. Viktor discovered our fundamental freedom, the one no one can take from us no matter what he or she does to us. People will do what they may, but they can't make us think in a certain way. Once we realize the way we think is our own essential freedom, our lives change dramatically. For Viktor, it struck him during a horrible point, and he thought, *You can do what you want to my body, but you cannot make me hate.* He focused on finding the beauty in life. He talked about how his ability to survive the horrors was helped when he was able to find the beauty in a meal consisting of a fish head floating in dirty water.

This was pivotal for me at the time, because if he could get through all that and come out of it as a successful doctor and author, conquering my issues seemed completely achievable. There may be no one or there may be twenty people ready to pull you out, but until you believe that you can do it, no change will occur. When someone helps you out, if the success of it all rests with the other person; you're going right back in because you aren't exercising your essential freedom. There is a difference between those who survive and flourish after going through so much and those who don't. It is not luck, magic, or station; it is belief.

Changing what you believe isn't an on/off switch. It takes work and self-awareness. Put the observer to work and check to see how many times a day you hook into thoughts of your own inadequacy. Correct them immediately with the truth, which is that you certainly can. These thoughts, which may have seemed appropriately humble and not conceited at first, have become beliefs of inadequacy, and know this: You cannot outperform your own self-image.

For some reason, it's easier to believe in the negative things about ourselves than the positive, so changing our self-image takes work. It's about working with our observer and being lovingly gentle with ourselves as we cycle through the process. In the beginning, we will forget about it sometimes, or we'll start working on it and all of a sudden realize that yesterday we went completely off the rails. It's okay. It's fine! Be as kind to yourself as you would be to a child learning to walk. Be loving, patient, and understanding with yourself. When the child stumbles, you would never be cruel to him. (If you would be cruel, put this book down and seek medical intervention right away. Otherwise, turn it all into a game, and experiment.)

The child never gives up trying to walk, and neither should you. It's a process, and just starting it will make things better. Check your beliefs and rewrite the programming that is running constantly in the background. You have the power because you truly are an intentional expression of love from the universe. You possess gifts; yes, you do, designed specifically to share with others. You may have completely suppressed your passions by believing you can never do anything with them. C'mon, let them out and play for a while. What do you have to lose? You are already cocreating your life. Try it against a better backdrop!

As an aware cocreator, you are an independent individual entitled to your own joy and wonder, as well as independent thought and independent action to pursue the passions dwelling deep within. Your joy and happiness are generated inside of you and not by exterior things. Sure, there are things that make us laugh or appreciate the textures, but true internal happiness comes from your internal belief: *I am a happy person*. It's a deeply rooted state of being and not an intermittent event.

You are a part of something vast and amazing. As a part of this infinite supply of potential, each of us must become independent of other people's opinions on what we can or cannot do, on what we should or should not do. Declare that you are an independent aspect of the whole, just as the universe designed you. Each of us is a separate and independent facet on a magnificent jewel, or think of it as being a wave in the ocean. Consider developing a belief that you will move into your potential. First, be independent in your thoughts. Do it with purpose. Select your direction and flourish in this gift of life with the blessings of your own unique passions. Trust that you are connected to and benefit from all that the universe offers from its infinite supply.

If beginning with the universal truth at the suggestion of this book leaves you uncomfortable, then begin with what Thomas Jefferson and his contemporaries believed when they wrote the Constitution of the United States.

CHAPTER 8

What Do You Think?

If you do what you always did, you will get what you always got.

—Anonymous

Don't believe everything you think.

—Byron Katie

As a man thinketh in his heart so is he.

—Proverbs 23:7

The combination of what we believe to be true and the intensity of our emotions linked to what we believe to be true is how we fully engage the universal mechanism that delivers more to us. If we generate negative emotions while we focus on all that we lack, we are sure to lack more. If we experience the joy in our hearts as we focus on gratitude for what we have, we get more of that as well.

Moving from being grateful for what we have to visualizing and stepping into the life in which we can flourish isn't that big a step. Take the time to imagine that life as you share your gifts, and revel in it as though it is already yours. And be intensely grateful for it.

This is how we create a new belief system, where we understand that when we believe it, we will, in fact, see it.

The hardest part of making a transition to living that amazing life is accepting the fact that as cocreators of our lives, we are accountable for the lives we are living now. So many people are victimized by their lives, moving through each day resigned to the belief that there isn't anything they can do about it. That's BS. If you believe it, that's your own BS. Simply put, what you believe to be absolutely true—so much so that you would defend it endlessly—is just a belief, nothing more. You believe it, so it is true for you. Why not play around a bit—start with something small and change one of your current beliefs?

Try something that can make your life better right now, something like no longer believing that when your boss asks you to take the minutes at a meeting, it just means he or she needs your assistance. Believe that the only thing your boss is thinking is ensuring adequate minutes are taken and you are the best person to take them. Stop thinking that the boss is demeaning you, taking advantage of you, or too lazy to do it. Just do it and be grateful for the opportunity to help make the meeting successful.

If there is something that you feel is impossible for you to do—for example, going back to school—try registering for a class and reset your belief system. Perhaps there is an art project calling you that you have believed up until now that you couldn't possibly produce. Get the materials and begin to play.

If you lack money, you're always thinking about how you can never get ahead, and you're frustrated and angry about that, you're ensuring that the circumstances will not change. Count your blessings. It's a real thing; do it! Whatever you do have—a leaky roof over your head, an old car, two cans of tuna and some noodles, or family—be grateful for them. Be grateful and expect that there will be more. Ask to be shown what your next step toward abundance can be, because changing your belief system is the first step. Stay open for the inspiration and ideas that will come your way. Then take a step; it doesn't have to be a big one. Just a step filled with intention.

There is a lot of information out there about affirmations and positive thinking. These are good things, yes, but, if you can't believe what you're saying about yourself, they don't help much. Saying something over and over that is opposite of what you truly believe doesn't take you very far. It does get you started. You have to build a road to believing it about yourself. Know and believe that you are an expression of the universe and that through your direct connection, whatever you choose to express is also part of God, good or bad, happy or sad, with no judgment to alter your free will. Ask and you will receive. It's how we actually ask that was the big surprise for me in all this.

As you express your gifts and passions, remember that you are directly connected to the infinite universal supply of love and possibility. The universe translates your feelings and the focus of your attention as the real representations of your desires.

The universe doesn't listen for your words; it is constantly receiving information from your beliefs, feelings, and emotions. It knows what you are focused on, constantly thinking about all the time. The areas where you focus your attention read as though they are what you intend to have in your life. You are constantly transmitting, and your signal is interpreted as, "More, more, more of this, please!" Be grateful not just for what you have, but for what you know you *will* have. Spend time each day reveling in a vision of that amazing life you're seeking, and see yourself there sharing your gifts, living a blessed life, and being a blessing to others.

Then there's the situation of low self-esteem. It is very personal. Although there may have been a causal event, the belief that you are less deserving, smart, or anything else than other people simply isn't true. You may immediately want to provide proof of your belief, but it's only true to the extent that you believe it to be true. This is your very own, tightly wrapped up BS that governs your life.

So, to you I say, pretend, just for a little while, that the universe created all of us, like a gigantic field of flowers, a huge earthly bouquet, and loved each and every one of us. The universe designed us to complement one another, to be key pieces of the bigger picture that no flower or bunch of flowers could see from this angle. Think about how you would feel if you were, in fact, an intentional and perfect universal expression on a path to be yourself as you serve the greater good by just being your perfect self, as you are.

What if you're on a journey of growth and you are exactly where you're supposed to be, and right now, it's time to see that we are all at exactly the same level but have different experiences, creating the infinite variety in this immense field? We have the same level of worthiness and are completely loved by the creator. You were set in motion, had experiences, and are here to serve a greater good by being you. How would this feel? Revel in that feeling and realize that it's true. Make this your belief system. Just for a time at first, play with it. See how you like it.

If you're thinking all this is good for some people, but your situation is different, I have to ask you, what if you only had to convince one person that these statements were true—just one? What if you just had to change just one person's mind? Yes, you are that person. Here is a little experiment.

Imagine that you are in complete control. Use your magic wand— go ahead! No one is looking!

And while you're there, you know for certain that you are an intentional expression of God, and along with your pulse and your breath and your life, you are entitled to everything you can use to live a fulfilling and joyful life.

There is no doubt at this moment. Feel what that feels like for a moment. If it doesn't come right away, think about how you would feel if there weren't any doubt. Imagine it, feel it, and experience the sensation.

Finally, I want to remind you of the beginning of this book and how I changed everything that was important around me at work by changing how I thought about it. I combined a real desire I had, to be a consultant, with looking at my environment through an entirely new lens. Granted, at the time, I thought I was moving from looking at life the way it really was to a sort of pretend environment, but in reality, I just changed lenses.

I went from a lens focusing on disrespect and frustration to one that focused on harmony and collaboration. My perception changed and served as the catalyst to change my world.

So, what do you think?

CHAPTER 9

Making Room

When you're working on getting more out of your life, be sure you have a place to put it!

—Dee G. Suberla

Let go or be dragged.

—Zen proverb

Before we get into going after what you want, we need to make a little room to put the wonderful things you'll be creating. Our minds are filled with all sorts of things, and some of them are working directly against what we truly desire. Let's bring a few of them out and shine that brilliant light of the loving universe on them. Perhaps we'll even get a few of them to evaporate and leave some perfectly good space for your heart's desires.

Some of the thoughts and beliefs that may be working against you are old grudges, guilt, and those old videos that we play over and over again. You know the videos we use to relive the pain of when someone hurt us. We not only hold on to these things; we re-experience them during each replay in our minds. The stress we suffer as a result is real. Our bodies don't really differentiate between what happens in real time versus what happens during the replay. The stress is the same, and the pain is the same, but the frustration that we didn't do something differently just increases our stress—and it is exhausting.

What if you, on your own, could stop reliving and restressing because of the replays? To be able to accomplish this, you have to have the desire to stop and the willingness to let it go, for real. It becomes a habit, which you will break with intention and effort. You might say, "Duh. Of course, I want it to stop, but biologically we're conditioned to repeat behaviors through a need to seek out what is familiar."

When freaking out is the norm, some amount of reflex has to be dealt with and managed. Pick something that isn't necessarily life-changing, just slightly irritating, to play with these concepts.

In his blog post, "The Significance of Letting Go," Omar Sharif shared the Zen proverb "Let go or be dragged." I love this because it is so true, and you can think of reliving something and suffering the responses over and over. Holding onto something negative is like being dragged along a rocky path, and there is only one way to stop it: let it go.

Whatever it is, it happened in the past, and as a result, no amount of thought, action, or worry will change it. It's done.

So, how do you put a stop to all that? To begin with, you have to be able to say, with complete honesty, that you want to let it go. You have to think it and say it out loud as support for overcoming that biological need to seek the familiar—in this case, your habit of suffering. If you want to stop reliving the pain, say it, write it, and look yourself in the eyes each morning and say it again. We're also dealing with that feeling that staying with the familiar is better than venturing out into the unknown. That fear is another trick to keep us exactly where we are, even though it simply doesn't feel good.

Things that are over and not present in this moment shouldn't be taking up prime real estate in your thoughts and making your body feel as though they are part of the present moment. They are not. They are just haunting replays. Start the process of letting things go by acknowledging that they happened, but without rerunning the tapes. Understand that at this point, they would just serve as a trap door dropping you back into the replay. Trap doors usually have the words *yeah, but* painted on them.

Whether you are trying to figure out why someone would do something like that or why you yourself would do something so dumb, it doesn't really matter right now. It's like spilled milk. We just need to wipe it up and toss the paper towel, not analyze why the glass fell over. It's done. Just know that the first step of moving on is what will be done today.

The next step is kind of a tough one. I'm going to use a word that might make you uncomfortable, but stay with me for the more universal definition. You move on—you recover your mental real estate—by forgiving. Yes, forgiving. Okay, take a minute to blow a gasket and come back to see what I really meant.

Welcome back. The idea of forgiveness has nothing to do with the person or people who hurt you. Yes, even if it is the you from the past that you must forgive. Forgiveness is done for one purpose only: to regain your power by taking the power away from the memory. You forgive yourself, or another, not because you've come to the conclusion that what happened was okay or right in any sense. (It was wrong.) You do it so you can let go and stop dragging yourself across the rocky path.

I have heard it said that holding on to your anger at someone, living or dead, for something he or she did to you in the past is like clinging to hot coals with the intention of throwing them into the face of your aggressor. Well, who's getting burned? I've also heard it's like drinking poison hoping to kill someone else. Again, who loses? Your anger, your frustration, and the feelings of betrayal are all just burning you from the inside out, and the only thing left to do is to forgive and move on. So, release connection to the person who betrayed you, fired you, hurt you. Set free that guilt from your mistake that everyone knew about; forgive yourself. Let go or be dragged.

This is, of course, a process. One way to start it is by wishing you could forgive the person who hurt you. Start with something small, or something that would be small if it didn't make you so darn angry! This is a place to start. Think about forgiveness as your vehicle to freedom for you. You might have to repeat the "I wish I wanted to forgive you" part quite a few times.

As you move forward, think about what it would be like if you didn't spend a single moment thinking about the event anymore. Tell me what that would feel like, out loud. I know, I can't hear you, but I'm not the point. Just imagine what it would feel like, and then give it "I would feel … I would no longer …"

One thing is certain: Whether you do or don't forgive the person, his or her life (or afterlife) isn't going to change. You're the one who is living the hell with the replay, not him or her. Just play with it and give yourself some time. At the very least, visualize what life would be like if you were set free of the emotional turmoil you suffer each time you think about it. It will cross your mind from time to time, but you are free of those caustic thoughts and feelings. Try to get there for a few moments, and then a day. If you can do it for a short time, then with practice, you can extend the amount of success you have. Don't assign a time line to it. Just plan to keep moving in that direction.

Do whatever you can do to let some old hurts go through forgiveness. I think that it's probably hardest to forgive ourselves. Try to see yourself as a different person. You aren't that person anymore, and given the same circumstance, you wouldn't do it again. You've lived and learned. Let it go, and think about helping others in some way rather than using all your power to beat yourself up. Research the success stories of people pulling themselves out of the depths of depression. The opposite of love is not hate; it's apathy. It's not caring at all.

To further support the concept of making space for something new, commit to clearing out the clutter, starting with a few small areas in your home. Combine the mental work with a little physical work. Clear out a drawer, a closet, or some other storage space. Recycle or discard those things that are no longer usable. Release those things that you aren't using, so they can bring joy to others, by donating them. Consider a garage sale to generate some money to help you take a step toward some element of the life you would love. Even small steps are taken by using your gift of free will. Use it to move you toward where you would really like to be.

CHAPTER 10

Using Your Magic Wand

People make basic assumptions based on what they have now. But you have to ask yourself, is this really what [you] are going to be doing in five years? Very few people ask themselves what they would actually want instead if they could wave a magic wand.

—Drew Houston,
Founder and CEO of Dropbox

Now I'd like to move into the mysteries of using your magic wand. I love to break out the trusty ole magic wand in my workshops. It's nothing extravagant. My favorite type of magic wand can be purchased for one dollar in the local craft store. If you're scrambling around frantically trying to find your magic wand, no worries; just use your imagination and your favorite pen. As you might have guessed, it's not really the tool that is important; it is your belief in the tool that makes all the difference.

The first thing you do to power up your magic wand is to suspend disbelief. In other words, disassociate from your own belief system for a few minutes. Be completely free of any doubt, of any linkages to what you know to be the facts at the moment. The best way to do this is to say, "Yep, it's time to play!"

To successfully describe your most fulfilling life, unchain your imagination. Just let it go for a little while. What is the silliest thing you can imagine? An elephant in a tree? Coughing up hummingbirds? Flying into outer space in your PJs? Take just a few minutes and imagine something fun, silly, and completely outrageous; then play with it a little bit.

How was that for you? Everything okay? You just imagined something and you came back, and you're okay—right? It's mind play, and it's a great exercise and something we can all do more often. Does it seem like folly? Wasted time? Well, Einstein thought the use of our imagination was pretty important. Just sayin', if it's good enough for him …

As you prepare to use your magic wand, it is important to remember a few things. First of all, you possess the magic. You are the engine for all the magic, and it happens when you throw the doors to your universal connection wide open! You know you've done it when you can imagine the rush of possibilities flowing all around you and find comfort in the knowledge that you wield the power in this magical place.

Second, there simply are no limits whatsoever related to the life you would love to be leading. The areas you might consider are health, relationships, earning a living, how you live, and where you live. Honestly imagine the life you want and include as many aspects of that life as you're comfortable with, or just start with one. Remember to open up to how your passions can help others. We've all been given different combinations of passions so that we can share them with others. You are blessed with your own set of passions, so don't minimize them.

The whole point of this exercise is to answer the question, "What does the life you would love look like?" What do you love? This goes beyond your favorite flavor of ice cream, of course. I'm talking about what you would really, really love to do with your precious moments, your life. For this, you must go deep inside and figure out what you would just absolutely love to do, or do more of—and remember, the focus is on you. Yeah, you heard me—just for you! If you begin to imagine your amazing life as one where everyone else is happy and living an amazing life but you haven't identified anything for yourself, you've entirely missed the point. You can imagine what it would look like so that you can do more for people, but that's it, my friend. This one is for you!

Third, as you're doing all this, generate a feeling of gratitude. Be thankful for what you have, who you are (yes, I'm not kidding about that), and the life you will lead in this exercise. Literally feeling the sense of gratitude is essential. If you are having feelings not in line with this, step away from the magic wand. You are playing with these feelings, so let yourself feel them; don't hold back. Remember, you can always go back to disbelief once the play is over. It's like diving into a beautiful pool of water that is the perfect temperature. You're in there for a while, but when you get out, you dry yourself off and go on to the next thing.

Finally, if you don't have the details of what your favorite life would look like, start by going through a list of things you do like—little things or big things. Your ability to imagine the things you really enjoy right now represents your passions. It can be figuring things out (puzzles or mysteries) or creating things (stories, blankets, birdhouses, wedding cakes). We're looking at simple pleasures where you find joy.

Consider having an imagining session before you wave that magic wand to create a view of things you really enjoy and imagine what things would look like if those expanded into a way of life, a place to live, or a unique job to earn a living. Imagining sessions work best when you write down what you find. First imagining, then feeling, and then writing it down creates a foundation. If there is even the slightest chance you will decide to move toward the life you most desire, take a generous amount of time to play with that vision, live in it for a while, and describe the life where you flourish, on paper. You see, it's just thinking and scribbling right now.

Just give it a try. Get comfortable and relax. Wave that magic wand and create the picture of the life you flourish in, the life you are so excited to be living, the life that you just absolutely love. What are you doing? What are you seeing? What are you feeling? Observe everything and stay with it as long as you can.

The whole purpose of the playing around is to come up with a destination, something you can see and describe. Because, as we all know, life is a journey. It's easier to take a journey when you know where the heck you are going. So, create your own utopia and don't worry about how it sounds to anyone else. You are providing a map to share with the universe so that your journey can now begin. When there are clear images combined with strong emotions like gratitude and joy, the universe works with you to make it happen. And you'll see it when you believe it!

Creating a picture of the life you love is an ongoing exercise. It's not a "one and done"! Nope, it's a continuous event. You get so far on the journey and one day you think, *Hey, wouldn't it be cool if this was there instead of that?*

Always remember, the universe hears us through our truest beliefs and gains clarity through the emotions we attach to them. Your strongest beliefs about your life are the areas that the universe continues to serve up for you. No judgment, no guidance, just answering your beliefs with events to enforce current circumstances matching up to those beliefs. I quote Dr. Dyer again: You'll see it when you believe it.

CHAPTER 11

The Questions You Ask

Set your ideal as near to perfection as your imagination is capable
of forming the conception.

—Wallace D. Wattles,
The Science of Getting Rich

I ran across an advertisement for a writer's conference on Maui, and I immediately wanted to be there. I had been to the Hawaiian Islands a few times in my life, but I've always wanted to spend some time on Maui. In the past, whenever I would see something advertising Maui, I would immediately think, *I'd love to go, but I can't afford it.* And that would be that; on to the next thing. In reality, I could afford it, but I always chose other priorities over the $1,200 airfare.

I had been studying this material for quite a while, so in this particular situation, when I saw the experts who were going to speak at this conference, my strong desire to go served as a reminder of what I had been teaching about how the quality of our lives can be affected by the questions we ask. It was time for me to "walk the talk." So, I asked the question, and I asked it big: "How can I get to Maui for free?"

I was excited about the possibilities of some gigantic move the universe would make to ensure I could go for free. I opened myself up to inspiration and new ideas, since I am fully aware that is how the universe communicates. Then I happily went on about my business.

And it worked. I flew to Hawaii for free, took part in the seminar, and loved every minute! The way I was able to do it was always available to me, but I had never considered it because before I had systematically turned off the hose that was always there, ready to feed me the inspiration and ideas. Turns out this particular possibility had been around me for quite a while. It was there all along. The answer was so simple. Less than two days later, I had an idea about the points on a credit card.

I do have a frequent flyer account with an airline that doesn't fly to Maui. I had never thought about those credit card points as part of the equation before. In the past, I made a feeble attempt to check them out a couple of times but was always distracted and didn't feel like spending the time to figure it out. I went quite a few years thinking that they had expired. Well, I was wrong; they didn't expire, and by combining those points and the miles from my usual airline, I was able to fly there for free. I flew to Maui and back, for free!

I have to acknowledge the importance of how simple the answer was and how I was thinking that the universe would have to make a big move to facilitate this idea. But in reality, the opportunity to fly for free had been there each and every time I assumed that I couldn't go to Maui because I couldn't afford the airfare. But—I had pinched off the inspiration. I didn't even ask the question. I just assumed there was no way. Actually, I had never even tried to imagine getting there for free before. Pinched it right off!

Another example: I was on an annual shopping trip with my friends. I had been reflecting on my upcoming wedding anniversary and thought about our honeymoon in Jamaica, where were first introduced to Blue Mountain coffee. It was delicious, and I wished I could buy some for my husband. It would be a wonderful gift, and I knew just the aroma of the brewing coffee would bring back memories of the beauty we had shared in Jamaica. It made me smile.

We were in one of those stores that carried mostly clothing and accessories, but in the back, they had a bunch of stuff, including food, on the shelves. I walked up to the first shelf, and my jaw dropped. There, on the top shelf, was a two-pound bag of Blue Mountain. I grabbed that bag, clutched it to my heart, and expressed my gratitude with tears in my eyes. Wow, it was so immediate!

One more story. Remember when I talked about taking that first class? My assignment was to write down a description, in as much detail as I possibly could, that represented the life I would love to live. I got pretty detailed, and it was a couple of pages, but it included being able to spend my winters out west and still have a home in northern Illinois. I'm writing to you from my home in Arizona right now. It's a long story, and I would be happy to share it with you sometime, but right now, I'll just take a piece of it to share.

My husband and I decided we had to try spending a few months out west during the winter. We found and rented a house in one of the towns near Phoenix. A couple of months after we made a deposit, the would-be landlords returned our check and told us they were selling the property. What? Did we just get fired from vacation? We made a joke about it, and then I said, "Let's see what other options we have." We discussed all the people we wanted to see out west. There was family in Texas, one in Arizona, and a few in California. The more we talked about it, the more it sounded as if we were looking for an RV life rather than renting one place. Maybe we needed to be looking at a motor home so we could hit the road and still have freedom to roam.

We looked at motor homes, and my husband and I were hit pretty hard by sticker shock. We weren't even sure we would like the RV life and didn't want to invest so much money. We decided to wait until things got cold before looking at anything else, assuming prices would drop. We also thought we should probably be looking at used RVs. I worked with my husband to define what sort of motor home we would like, but he was still concerned about the pricing. I asked him to stop assuming it would be too expensive and instead to come up with the amount we would be comfortable with. This took some coaxing, mind you, but we had time.

So as the snow flurries started, we headed back to the place we wanted to buy from. They started us with some pricy and beautiful RVs and we told the salesperson that we didn't want to pay that much. We described what we wanted, and he said, "Oh, one came in yesterday on a trade in that sounds like what you're looking for. It hasn't been cleaned yet, but let me go get the keys."

We looked at it, and it was, in fact, what we were looking for, and the price actually shocked my husband. It was right where we wanted it. I'll never forget the expression on his face when he looked me in the eye and said, "This %$#& universe really works!"

I have more stories, but what is important to remember is that there are billions and gazillions of things happening and existing all the time. We are not able to see, experience, or even imagine them all at once. When we get specific about what we want to achieve or be or do, there is a whole universe of possibility there to support us and help us connect with what is out there. But we have to open up to it. We have to be clear and lovingly connected to it. And for me, I have to have a generosity of spirit to go along with it to truly resonate with my sense of purpose. It has to include sharing and doing for others. That's why I wanted to go to that writers' conference. I wanted to create a book combining the ideas in the materials I was researching and introduce them with real-life examples using a "how to" approach, So, again I say to you, "Ta-da!"

CHAPTER 12

Respond or React: Choose One

Your problem isn't the problem. Your reaction is the problem.

—Anonymous

Be miserable. Or motivate yourself. Whatever has to be done, it's always your choice.

—Dr. Wayne Dyer

When something occurs, we respond. An event doesn't carry with it a package of emotions; those belong to people. An event happens, and we respond to it. We immediately decide whether it's good or bad, and then we react accordingly.

There is an instant between the happening and the responding that most of us don't notice, ever. We just react and react. Let's say there is a teenager living with you who just cannot stop leaving the hairbrush on the kitchen counter. You have told this teen a thousand times to stop doing that because nobody wants hair where they eat! Over time, you are very nearly driven crazy by this habit, and each time you approach the kitchen, you begin to crouch and slowly peek around the corner to see if it happened again. Yep, it did, and in a fury, you grab that brush and hurl it outside, in the teen's room, in the garbage can—or maybe you break it in half while screaming, "*Argh!*"

I submit to you that you and your observer can come up with a team solution to this problem. This is a great example to use to begin working with your observer and your reactions and responses. The next time you are approaching the kitchen, just boldly walk in and understand that the brush may or may not be there. As you move your eyes around to see, check in with your observer, who is probably saying something like, "No, we are looking to see if the brush is there." It is there. *Cut:* This is that instant where you can choose to react or respond. Up until now, you have been reacting. You did not engage your higher brain functions for even a second. You just went to what is called your reptilian brain. Think, caveman brain.

Since then, our brains have developed, and we now have a frontal cortex, which we use to assess and strategically consider options. Reactions pinch off our ability to think strategically in a calmer manner. In that instant, if you are tracking with your observer, who isn't connected to emotions, you can choose how you will respond this time. You can ignore it, break it, throw it, call the teen into the kitchen and have him remove it, take a picture and post it on Facebook, or choose some other response. When you choose to respond, you take action without dumping all kinds of adrenalin and cortisol into your bloodstream that will stay with you a good portion of the day, accelerating your heartbeat and perhaps helping you to obsess on the craziness of the whole situation—*again.*

You have probably heard of the fight-or-flight response. When it is triggered, our bodies will be flooded with a bath of chemicals to prepare us to fight for our lives or to run and get the heck out of there. We hear stories of people lifting cars off loved ones or other feats of strength.

Unfortunately, we have a tendency to trigger that response at other times that don't really involve any need whatsoever for the chemical dump. We trigger it if someone is driving too slow in front of us, or too fast in back of us. And look out for those poor folks who have the audacity to cut us off! Other times, we engage this lifesaving cocktail in reaction to something someone said about us behind our back, or when our boss asks us to do something we hate doing—or when someone leaves a brush on the kitchen counter.

When someone is doing or saying something that normally makes you mad, walk with your observer. Commit to responding, rather than reacting. Give yourself the courtesy of engaging your strategic thinking. You may decide that you are angry, but you can respond more calmly and actually make sense. You can ask questions and learn more.

How it usually works is you decide you're going to work on responding rather than reacting. Then something happens, and after losing it and calming down, you remember, *Oh, darn! I was supposed to respond.* After a couple of those, you will remember immediately afterward, and then perhaps while doing it. Eventually, you remember to do it before reacting. All of it is good. Let yourself play with this idea.

If you are the kind of person who gets angry at the ridiculous stupidity that seems to surround you in the world, you might want to check into some of the biological research on why you're doing that. There are biological causes for us to do the same sorts of things over and over. There are parts of our makeup that want to stick with the familiar and will work to make sure we stay with "what works."

Oddly enough, if you are an overreactor, suffering from three, four, or more angry outbursts a day, there is a biological cause, and you need to work to override it for your own sake. You're on a sort of treadmill of emotions because … well, because that's what you've always done. If we were talking about it right now, face to face, I think you might suggest that you can't help it, that there are just so many idiots out there and you just don't tolerate that kind of stupidity … or something like that.

Baloney! Each outburst is flooding your body with the chemical cocktail designed to save your life, and you are overdoing it, which leads to a less-than-healthy system over the years. Remember that there are millions of people out there, and if you're drawn to the idiots all the time, well, then let's just say you are looking for them, you are expecting them, and each and every encounter is proof positive that they're overrunning the earth!

Sure, people do stupid or even idiotic things. They also make mistakes or different choices. Not everything you see is exactly as you would describe it. Biologically, you are poised and waiting for that next piece of proof, and you'll go a long way to find it. Maybe someone is stopped at a cross street and you're trying to let him out, but he ignores you and doesn't show any appreciation for your generosity. What an idiot! Or maybe he just got news of something horrible. Maybe he has forgotten something important and is thinking of backing up and going home to get it. Maybe, just maybe, you are not in any way related to what or why people are doing what they're doing.

When we operate from habit or assumptions, we not only pinch off our strategic thinking, but also pinch off our observer and the universe. There is so much more there for you; play around with finding your own way to access it.

Much of our anguish and instinctual reactions can also come from judging people or arguing against something that has happened. An event occurred; it happened and it's done, and we spend time raging against the fact that it happened. It can be that you were disrespected by someone who just doesn't like you, or you could have been fired for no reason, or the worst would be that a loved one passed away.

Check out the work of Byron Katie, an author and speaker who teaches a method of self-inquiry she calls "the Work." She feels that all our suffering is caused by arguing with what is. When something has happened, there is no going back. In many cases, we do need to have room to adjust, assess, or mourn, but if we stop raging against the fact that it happened, we will be able to respond appropriately. If you think about how much pain and misery we put ourselves through by obsessing about the injustice of something that has happened, it's shocking. Once you accept that it happened, you can move into dealing with it. Deal with it and begin the healing process; move forward.

We must all remember that our belief system (BS) is an internal concept. What we believe to be true is not necessarily a universal fact. It may be what we know inside, but our beliefs are our own and they are not the beliefs of all.

Each of us is on a path of spiritual exploration, and when something happens that is not in line with our own BS, it doesn't mean it is out of sync with the universe. In fact, whatever happens is in sync with the universe, and it's not our job to judge, rage against, approve, or otherwise manage it. We must process and move on over time or in the moment, whatever is appropriate. No matter how we manage to do this, it is entirely our choice.

We must proceed by decision, not by instinct. In doing so, we are able to fully engage the sense God gave us and ensure that the next step serves the greater good. Sometimes, just letting it go and turning away is the answer. Raging over things we cannot control is like hitting ourselves in the face with a hammer every time we don't like what someone else is doing.

So, from this moment on, based on the information here (and the assumption that you're still with me), you are choosing not to overreact to events in your life. Work with your observer and override the biological habit that was designed to keep you near the cave and not wandering off.

CHAPTER 13

Now, Just Take a Step

Work consists of whatever a body is obliged to do. Play consists of whatever a body is not obliged to do.

—Mark Twain

We don't stop playing because we grow old; we grow old because we stop playing.

—George Bernard Shaw

Play is the only way the highest intelligence of humankind can unfold.

—Joseph Chilton Pearce

And so, I say, "Play!"

Whether I am training clients in project management, leading an organizational development workshop, or even coaching a client, there is always that question: "So, how I do I actually start this?" In corporate America, I suggest they pilot a few of the procedures, and in coaching, I say, *"Play!"* Bam! You've been coached!

When you are making changes, your starting mindset is everything. There is a lot here that you can try. You don't have to do everything according to a recipe. Do it according to what pulls at you a little bit. Listen to your inner voice. You will be learning and changing and growing no matter which steps you choose to help yourself; just keep your eye on the target. It's not time for linear thinking; pick and choose based on how it feels. The order of your choices, or the choice to play with a few of these ideas simultaneously, will never be a mistake. There are no mistakes; it's all just information for fun.

Allow yourself time to play and change and reorganize. Use what you learn, and have fun while you move toward your dreams. It's all based on what you're thinking *plus* how you are thinking about what you're thinking. Okay, you might need to reread that a couple of times. I love this quote: "A man's way of doing things is the direct result of the way he thinks about things."[2]

I frequently paraphrase by saying, "The way you live your life is the direct result of how you think about your life." If you take nothing else away from this book, please take that message. Once you realize that you have so much more control over yourself than you ever realized, you can start playing your way to get anywhere you choose in life. But before that can happen, my friend, *you must be willing to play.*

People frequently share their stories of troubling situations in which they concluded from the words and actions of other people that they are in some way broken, worthless, or stupid. The importance of being willing to play for these people—and let's face it, for most of us—is to experience the liberation of thinking wonderful things about ourselves. After living a long time thinking negative things about ourselves, it

---

[2] Wallace D. Wattles, *The Science of Getting Rich* (Virginia: Thrifty Books, 2009), 16.

is so hard to actually think something wonderful. But if we convince ourselves that, at first, we are just playing, we can sample how it feels.

Try creating a phrase like this: "I am an amazing, intentional creation of the loving universe. I have much love to give and am ready, willing, and able to receive all the love the universe has for me." Or "I am perfect just the way I am at this moment. As I move forward, I'll make even better choices."

I don't mean to get you started on affirmations, even though the phrase you create may very well be an affirmation. I want you to make believe that you believe these words completely, even for just a minute or two. Then ask yourself, "What would it be like if it was true?"

Take a few minutes to think about that. *What if it was true? What would my life be like if it was true? How would I feel tomorrow as I wake up if this was true? How would I go about tackling work that needs to be done?*

What could possibly make it be true for you? You.

Just play with a few ideas or concepts. Okay, fine, I'll share my own on-ramp to finding something better. I have always loved photography but have hated having my picture taken. Anytime I saw a picture or a reflection of myself, I would respond with thoughts or words along the lines of, "You're disgusting!" Now, there are all sorts of ways to say and think that, and believe me, I found a lot of them.

So, back to "walking the talk." I decided to play with it and pretend to believe it. So, every time I saw myself, I would say "Look at you— you're as cute as a bug's ear!" Or "What a doll. You're beautiful." Trust me, I laughed a lot because, after all, I have complete respect for playing! One day, while washing my hands, I looked in the mirror and thought, *Hey, I look pretty good today.* It was spontaneous and honest and, most importantly, something I really felt. And then, boy oh boy, did I laugh. Since then, I've taken up the habit of reminding others of how cute I am today.

Do I slip up sometimes and dive under a table when the cameras come out? Sure. But I get back on track. The key mechanism of success here is deciding how I want to think about my life versus just thinking the same things I've always thought because, well, that was the way I've always thought. Back then, I would follow up with, "but it's not my fault!" Saying that it's not my fault doesn't change a thing; it just cements the negative thoughts in a little further because it means I'm a victim of my own life.

Counter that by recognizing and taking accountability for what you think about yourself. Choose to believe some old, worn-out, crummy recordings in your head, or choose something better. While playing with the concept, choose something small and really play with it.

Another area I play with is recognizing when I run into one of those situations where I react without thinking. The thrill of recognizing this before opening my mouth is one of the most treasured gifts that I received from these materials. Admittedly, I am not always successful, but I have improved. It is a wonderful experience to realize that I can keep my reactions in check when I hear something that upsets me, versus saying something stupid because I misunderstood what the other person said. Now I stop and ask clarifying questions, or ask him or her to say it a different way because I'm not sure I caught the meaning. Humiliation via my own mistakes has been one of my very best teachers.

My ability to deal with my anger used to come up more than I care to admit in my work and personal life. Most of the situations had nothing to do with me. I would get all worked up about someone else's path, words, or actions that had nothing at all to do with me. Recently, I saw a saying I love: "Not my circus, not my monkeys." Yes, I'm still dealing with being a Judgie McJudger but it gets a lot easier to laugh at myself when I realize I'm doing it again. I have to say that when I do get into trouble, it's usually because I'm taking myself way too seriously.

As a reformed victim, I can tell you that it does take work to get started. And that work is mostly thinking on purpose and against the established grain. But *wow,* how liberating once you focus on living your own life the way you want to live it. It is a process that bears fruit intermittently at first. There is no straight line to perfection. Heck, you're already perfect; you just don't see it yet. Begin to live it by just imagining it: a life where you focus on creating your own joy and happiness, a life where you expect to see and feel the wonder and love that is already there for you, a life where you share your passions and know your very own inner peace. And you laugh and laugh and laugh! Hey! Can I get a giggle?

C'mon, let's play!

CHAPTER 14

Tools, Tips, and Tidbits

I couldn't close off until I shared a few things that might help you out, should you choose to play. I'm providing potentially inspirational grids to help organize your thoughts about the life you would love to live. These are just starting points. You are free to organize your thoughts any way you want. Remember that writing it down helps you obtain clarity. Think it, say it, and write it for the best outcomes.

Tools
Finding My Passions

Use this to give yourself an idea of what your real passions are. This isn't in order of priority, and it isn't based on anything you've ever been told. My go-to example is this: if you want to be a cheerleader on the international space station, write that down! Use a form like this or create a journal. There's no rush; take a lot of time and be selective with what you list here. Dig deep. When you can find something that you would really love to do (or do more of), write it down. *Do not* dissolve it by saying those infamous words, "But I can't because … blah, blah, blah" (see rule 6 at the end of this chapter). Just play with the things you love and remind yourself of those things you would prefer to have less of in your life.

Use this list for guidance when asking yourself questions such as, "Hmm, what should I be when I grow up?"

Random things I love to do	Stuff I avoid if I can

My Reaction Triggers

When these things happen, I react without thinking and get angry.	Moving forward, I will create a pause to give myself time to plan my response (list examples)

Assumptions I Make When Thinking About My Life

This is intended to help you see the limitations you are putting on yourself. It is based on the concept that the way you think about your life is the way you live your life. Your assumptions about what you can't do (but really want to) throw you out of the realm of possibility for that simple reason: you believe you can't, and so you can't. Remember, if anyone ever has done this, you can do this too.

If you think of something you'd love to accomplish or experience and then immediately list all the reasons why you can't, see rule 6 at the end of this chapter. Stop trying to figure out how to do something—that part isn't up to you. Your job is to open yourself up to the universe of possibilities.

When you find something you'd like to do but always assumed that you couldn't, add it to this next table.

Living the Dream

Use this table to make notes on those things that would be present in your life when you are really living the dream! Consider writing it up or making a vision board by cutting out pictures and sayings representing what you would love and making a collage. It's all about making it real! You are making the targets you want to hit (no worrying about how you'll do it). List what you want and do not list anything that starts with these words or phrases: *not, I don't want, never.* Those are things you don't want. They don't belong here.

Example for relationships: harmony and humor; affectionate; constructive conflict; mutual respect; etc.

When I'm living the dream, these will be present in my life:					
Relationships	Health	How I earn	Where I live	What I see, do, feel	How I serve
Relationships include romantic, family, friends work, pets...					

Tips

- As you begin, don't look for validation from others. After all, you're just playing, right? In the beginning, it is a mistake to solicit advice from anyone who tells you what you are capable of or what you should really want, or who thinks that he or she knows what's really best for you (unless you are still a child, in which case, go read a Dr. Seuss book).

- Purposeful thinking takes focus. Mindless and sometimes cruel mind chatter is what happens when things have been on autopilot too long. Take the helm and focus on play. Have you heard the term *hard at play*? That's what I'm talkin' about!

- Never, ever, ever berate yourself again. Employ the old guidance of "If you can't say something nice, see rule 6 at the end of this chapter!" Treat yourself the way you would treat someone you love so much that you would give your life for him or her. 'Cause, in this case, that's who you are. When you get off track, guide yourself back. If you start with the negative talk, tell yourself to see rule 6 at the end of this chapter!

- If things get a little rough inside your own head and it's difficult to find a way out, go help someone else with something. Leave the house with the single purpose of looking for an opportunity to serve. Open a door for someone. Pay for the next person's coffee. Make eye contact with someone and smile. Compliment someone. Try thanking anyone serving you, and call him or her by the name on the name tag. Just open up to the idea that you're here to help. The opportunities are endless.

Author's Tidbits

These are some of my own personal rules to live by. I find them to be helpful and true for me. Create some for yourself or borrow some of mine. They can help you to navigate your way when things get complicated.

1. Take care of Number One first, because if you don't, you'll become useless to the rest of us.
2. If it ain't no fun, don't do it.
3. The guilty are the first to accuse.
4. Don't waste today worrying about tomorrow.
5. The quickest way to prevent learning is to be angry.
6. Note to self: Shut up!
7. We are *they.*
8. I can do anything I set my mind to. (Advice my mother gave me eight-thousand-plus times in my life—thank you, Mom.)
9. Be open to the possibilities.

10. Life is short. When all else fails, have fun, do good, and be kind.

11. Not making a choice is a choice and is almost always the wrong one.

12. I cannot grow beyond my expectations for myself, so keep 'em high, high, high!

I wish you all the best, and I hope you play with these ideas. So long for now. You can always find me on Facebook and LinkedIn, or even on my website, SuberlaConsulting.com. Go on now; have some fun!

Printed in the United States
By Bookmasters